W9-AYE-070

An Angel to Watch Over Me

An Angel to Watch Over Me

True Stories of Children's Encounters with Angels

Joan Wester Anderson

Ballantine Books • New

Library of Congress Cataloging-in-Publication Data
An angel to watch over me : true stories of children's encounters
with angels / Joan Wester Anderson.
p. cm.
ISBN: 0-345-38815-1
1. Angels. 2. Visions in children. 3. Children—Religious life.
I. Title.
BT966.2A515 1994
291.2'15—dc20 94-15722

Illustrations by Crista Abvabi

Text design by Holly Johnson

Manufactured in the United States of America

First Edition: September 1994

10 9 8 7 6 5 4 3 2 1

To my guardian angel.

Through the years, I have often lost sight of you.

But you have never forgotten me.

Acknowledgments

I would like to thank the following people for their help and encouragement. I am grateful to Steve Edwards of the Kristone Corporation in Tempe, Arizona; Sister Mary Christelle, BVM, of Wright Hall in Chicago; Salome Joseph of Elgin, Illinois; and Evelyn Heinz of McHenry, Illinois; all of whom tracked down some angel poems and sheet music for me. Also helpful was Sister Phyllis Vella of Holy Innocents School in Neptune, New Jersey, who located a hard-to-find interviewee.

I appreciate fellow author Ethel Pochocki Marbach of Brooks, Maine, who generously shared background material. Mark Overton of the Spoleto Festival in Charleston, North Carolina, as well as researchers at Chicago's Harold Washington Library, the Atlanta, Georgia, police department, and Word Publishing in Waco, Texas, deserve mention. I am grateful to the family of Mary Wadham and to Donna Boyd, for allowing me to use poems they have written. And a special thanks to Crista Abvabi, who drew the illustrations for this book.

Finally, I would like to thank the children who live on my street, as well as the children who wrote to me from across the country, all requesting angel stories about kids. May this book be as much a blessing to them as it has been to me.

Contents

Contents

xii

An
Angel to
Watch
Over Me

A Word About Angels

According to Scripture and tradition, God made angels before He created the world. Judaism, Christianity, and Islam all accept the existence of angels in varying degrees. Angels are a separate creation from humankind, spirits without bodies, although on occasion they take on physical form. They have three main functions: to worship God, to act as messengers between heaven and earth, and to guard humankind.

Although interest in angels has declined during the past few decades, there's been a recent resurgence, especially among the young. In 1988, a Gallup poll found that 75 percent of thirteen-to-eighteen-year-olds believed in angels, a gain of 10 percent since 1978. That number is probably even higher now. Even more interesting, a growing number of children and adults say they have *encountered* angels, either seeing or hearing them, or sensing their nearness in some special way.

This is really not as unusual as it seems, for traditionally, many of the world's religions recognize children's intrinsic awareness of and connection with the divine. The prophet Isaiah envisioned a welcome era when warring factions would lay down their arms and "a little child shall lead them" (Isaiah 11:6). Jesus cautioned against hindering children, "for to them belongs the kingdom of heaven" (Matthew 19:14). Teachings of the Church of the Latter-day Saints suggest that newborns have already lived in heaven and bring that awareness to earth when they arrive; ancient Egyptian hieroglyphics, as well, refer to children who have died as "returning to whence they came."

Culturally, too, youthful spirituality is considered natural and desirable. The Native American tradition is rich with stories honoring childhood visions and dreams. In some African tribal initiations, a vision or spiritual occurrence to a youngster is not only accepted but *expected*. In *Memoirs of a Quaker Boyhood*, Rufus Jones recalls, even as a young child, experiencing "a sense of divine presence" in the traditional Quaker silence. Sofia Cavalletti, a Montessori educator, believes that up to the age of seven or eight, children's prayers are "almost exclusively thanksgiving and praise," revealing their basic trust in the Creator. In the three most well-known Marian apparitions to date—at Fatima, Lourdes, and Medjugorje in the former Yugoslavia—the visionaries have all been children or young adults.

Even in the volumes of data surrounding near-death experiences, children seem to accept heavenly encounters with far more equanimity than adults. It is only as children grow older that such innate spiritual awareness seems to fade away.

A special note to parents: Little ones do appear to have a special bond with heaven. Perhaps it's because they haven't yet experienced a clear division between the two worlds and, for a little while, can be a part of each. You may have noticed this unique situation. Perhaps your preschooler has insisted that her "imaginary companion" is *real*, telling you of a time when she saw "a pretty lady in my room," or seemed to know something spiritual without you recognizing *how* she would know that. If such things happen to your child, be matter-of-fact and interested rather than negative or worried. If her observations are especially intriguing, you might want to write them down. Children often forget these episodes as they grow older, but a written record may serve to mark the experience as a special gift, a touchstone of faith.

If your child has never shown any interest in the heavenly host, you might want to whet his curiosity. For, no matter how loving and wholesome your home is, these are difficult times for your child. TV and movie violence is frequent—and often frightening. There are few adults that you can trust to care for him if he's worried or hurt. Perhaps he plays with children whose parents are involved in occult practices in their homes or whose behavioral standards are not as firm as yours. Some children must also cope with gangs and danger on the street. Your child might like to learn that angels exist, and that he can speak to them in his heart whenever he needs companionship or comfort.

Try it. Teach your child the angel prayers and songs you'll find in this book. Put a picture of an angel in his room, or hang up one that he drew (many parents say this is a sure cure for nightmares!). When she leaves for school or play, bless her and ask the angels to encircle her. When wonderful things unexpectedly happen during the day, share and celebrate them with your child. Soon the angels will become a natural part of life. "There are five of us in this family," one mother pointed out, "but I like to think that there are ten of us living in our house."

Make the angels welcome in your house, too.

A special note to children: In the beginning, before He created us, God made angels. Angels are pure spirits—they do not have physical bodies. They adore God in heaven, and do whatever He asks them to do.

There are different kinds of angels. Some are more important and are called archangels, as is the case with Gabriel and Michael. Others are sent by God to earth to be our guardians and friends.

When God made you, He told his angels, "Take care of this child." And the angels obeyed. This means that at least one special angel is close to you all the time, and others come when you need extra help and love. Angels go everywhere you go. They watch you when you play hide-and-seek or dry the dishes or go to school. They cheer you on when you're in a baseball game or practicing the flute. They sit by your bed if you're sick, and guard you when you're sleeping. Even when it's dark outside, they can see you.

Some children say they have seen or felt angels around them. Others have been rescued or protected by people who quickly disappeared—maybe these were angels in disguise! However, this is unusual. Most often, angels remain invisible (even though they are nearby), and so we must believe in them without actually seeing them.

When you are lonely or frightened, talk to your guardian angel. You can do it out loud, or inside your head—your angel can hear you whenever you speak. Ask your angel to be near you, to put his or her hand on your shoulder, to give you courage and protect you.

At other times, just enjoy the company of angels. And ask God to let you know more about these wonderful beings.

Dress Rehearsal

Twelve-year-old Dolores and her family were moving to a great but unusual house in San Antonio, Texas. It was L-shaped, and the smaller wing contained just two rooms: a recreation room with sliding glass doors that led onto a patio, and an isolated bedroom with its own space heater that could only be reached through a passageway leading from the rec room.

Her parents would probably take that out-of-the-way bedroom for their own, but Dolores longed to have it. As the oldest of seven children, she never seemed to have any privacy. She currently shared a room with a younger sister who was always messing up her stuff. And her brothers would barge in at the worst times, asking, "Can you play baseball, Dolores?" Or they'd yell, "Who are you talking to?" while she was on the phone. She loved her brothers and sisters, but they just didn't understand.

But her parents had a surprise for her. "The room in the smaller wing will be yours," they told their delighted daughter on moving day. "You deserve a little solitude."

Dolores happily settled into her new living arrangement. The rec room, of course, was noisy all day—everyone played there or watched television. But after dinner, when the family settled down to read or do homework, things grew quiet in her wing. Dolores was never nervous about being away from everyone else. She enjoyed her peaceful surroundings.

One evening, Dolores was lying on her bed reading, when all at once she felt as if she was being watched. She looked up at the little window. Its curtains were closed, and everything seemed secure. Then she looked over at her bedroom door.

In the doorway, *filling* the doorway, was a luminous figure, obviously looking at her. Dolores stifled a scream, for somehow she knew there was nothing to be afraid of. *Who are you?* she asked silently.

There was no answer, but Dolores felt a sense of happiness and well-being. The figure was, well . . . *nice.* Then, as she watched, it seemed to dissolve, "kind of like what happens to the people on *Star Trek* when they go into the transporter," she says.

Dolores lay awake for a while that night, trying to re-create the scene. Had it been a trick of light? No, for the figure had been there long enough for her to know it was real. Then why had it come? What was the point? She didn't know.

The next night, as Dolores sorted her clean laundry on the bed, the same feeling stole over her. Someone was watching her. Slowly she turned. The shining shape was back at the door. Dolores felt the same sense of contentment again when she saw the figure. *Why are you here?* she asked in her mind.

The apparition answered in the same way, without sound. *Follow me,* it said.

Why? Dolores asked.

Follow me. You are safe. Everything will be all right.

Slowly Dolores walked toward the figure. It turned and led her into the passageway toward the rec room, lighting up the dark narrow area as it went. But when Dolores reached the rec room, the shape had disappeared again.

Dolores tossed and turned that night. *Everything will be all right,* her unusual visitor had told her. But everything was all right *now.* What did the figure mean? And who was it?

The following night Dolores watched her doorway, but the luminous apparition did not come. She didn't know whether to be relieved or sorry when she finally turned off the light and crawled into bed.

But was she dreaming now? There seemed to be smoke, and a crackling sound. . . . It was so very hard to breathe. Suddenly she was choking, coughing. . . .

And there was the figure again, calling her with words she could hear in her heart: *Come, follow me. Everything will be all right.* Somehow Dolores was stumbling after the light as it led her down the passageway. She was gasping for air, crying. . . .

"Dolores!" she could hear her mother screaming as the patio doors rolled open and a man, wearing something that felt rubbery, reached in and grabbed her.

"She's all right!" the person was shouting, placing Dolores in the arms of her father and mother. Why, it was dark and the whole family was outside!

"We thought you were trapped in your room." Her mother was weeping while her father held her tightly. "How did you escape? There's smoke everywhere."

Escape? Dolores wondered what they were talking about. But her head was clearer now, and it was easier to breathe. She could see flames shooting through the rec room, firefighters aiming streams of water through the open patio doors. The L-wing was on fire!

"Looks like that space heater was defective," reported the fireman who had lifted her out. Puzzled, he looked at Dolores. "But the heater flames engulfed your bedroom doorway *first*. How did you get out of the room without being burned? And how could you have found your way down that dark passage to the patio doors? Even if you were still conscious, the smoke was too dense—you couldn't have seen anything."

Her father had a strange look on his face, too. "I awakened first," he told Dolores, "but only because *you* called to me. 'Daddy, get up,' you said. Yet I couldn't have heard your voice. You were much too far away."

Everything is going to be all right. And suddenly Dolores knew how, and

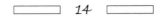
why, and even *who*. "My guardian angel had known what was going to happen," she says, "and he came early to prepare me to follow him—kind of like a dress rehearsal."

And she follows him still.

Never Alone

Five-year-old Carole was playing hide-and-seek with several neighborhood children. It was a fine day, sunny with a light breeze. But Carole wasn't having much fun. She was the youngest, and whoever was "It" always seemed to locate her first. It wasn't fair.

The next game was beginning. Where could Carole hide? Then she remembered the porch behind her house. *They'll never find me if I go under there!* she thought.

The porch was raised slightly to allow access to a cistern underneath

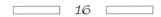
it. (A cistern is an underground tank that holds rainwater.) There was a fence built almost against the porch, but Carole was so tiny that she squeezed around it and crawled underneath the porch. There was the cistern, just ahead. Carole had never really looked down into it, she realized. Since she had to stay here until someone found her, now would be a good time to explore.

There was barely room under the porch for her to sit up, but she managed to drag the heavy lid off the cistern. Then, lying on her tummy, she looked inside it. Dark . . . Was there water down there? Carole inched a bit farther for a better view—and suddenly tumbled over the edge!

She screamed as she hit bottom, at least six feet down. Fortunately, the cistern was dry. She got up carefully. No, she didn't seem to be injured. But the hole was small—and what if there were spiders down here? "Help!" Carole yelled. "I'm stuck!"

Who would hear her, at the bottom of a hole under a porch? Although her eyes were becoming accustomed to the darkness, she could see practically nothing.

"Carole! Carole!" her friends were shouting.

"Here I am!" she called back. "In the cistern!"

But they were too far away. Time passed, and Carole heard them again. Now she recognized her mother and father's voices, along with those of the parents of her friends. "Carole! Carole, where are you?" It seemed that everyone was looking for her.

"Here, under the porch!" she yelled again and again. But no one came. Carole had tried to be brave, but now she started to cry.

And then she sensed a warmth around her, a reassuring presence. As if she was not alone. As if someone was in the cistern with her, knowing how she felt, telling her, without words, that everything was going to be just fine.

Carole's heart stopped pounding, and her tears dried on her cheeks. Who was it? She knew she was alone in the cistern—there wasn't room here for another person—yet she felt wrapped in a blanket of consolation and love. *Will you get my daddy for me?* she asked the presence silently.

Soon, the presence answered.

Carole sat down slowly. She felt comforted. She would wait.

More time passed. Then, abruptly, Carole heard her father's voice, very close. "She's under here—I know she is!"

"Daddy, Daddy!" she called. "Here I am!"

Her father's head appeared at the top of the hole. "Carole! Thank God." His hands were reaching down for her, touching her fingertips, then moving around her, pulling her up, up . . . and into his arms. Dragging her out from under the porch, he sat with her in the backyard as her mother and all the neighbors came running. Why, it was dark outside, and everyone had flashlights! "Oh, Carole." Daddy rocked her as his tears fell onto her cheeks. "We've been looking for you for hours . . . combing the woods, going up and down the state highway. . . ."

For hours! It had seemed only minutes! "How did you find me?" she asked.

"We regrouped here in the yard, to decide where to go next," Daddy said. "And then . . . and then I felt a force inside me, telling me to go and look past that little fence. I pulled it back and saw the open cistern under the porch. I never would have thought to look there, never in a thousand years, if I hadn't felt that . . . that . . ."

Carole laid her head on his shoulder. She knew. She had felt it, too.

☐

"Mom, can I go outside and ride my bike?" seven-year-old Aaron asked.

"Well . . ." Aaron's mother, Wendy, looked at the clock. The family was leaving for church services in less than an hour, and she needed to get Aaron's little brother ready. "Will you stay right in front of the house—and not get dirty?"

"Sure." Aaron slammed the door behind him, running to get his black-and-red bike.

Wendy smiled. Aaron probably *wouldn't* stay clean. But it was far too beautiful a day for a boy to be stuck inside.

A half hour passed, and Wendy went to the door. "Aaron! It's almost time to go!" she called. Aaron didn't answer. She looked up and down the street, but there was no sign of him.

Strange. Perhaps he had gone to his best friend's house on the next block. "We'll pick him up on our way," she decided.

Aaron's grandmother drove up, and everyone got into her car. But Aaron was not at his friend's house. No one there had seen him all afternoon. "Let's ask the other children," Wendy suggested, frowning. This was not like Aaron at all.

Aaron's grandmother drove up and down several streets, but although many children were outside and everyone knew Aaron, no one had seen him. "Where could he be?" Wendy wondered, worried. They returned home, and she called her husband, Glenn, at work.

Glenn came home right away. By now several people had gathered in front of the house. "Let's all spread out and look," a neighbor suggested. Glenn and some of the men rang doorbells, and inspected garages and yards. Someone else drove back to the neighborhood where the family used to live. Mothers put their babies in strollers and walked up and down the streets, calling, "Aaron!" But Aaron seemed to have vanished.

Eventually, Wendy and Glenn phoned the police. Two officers came and took a report. Tears spilled down Wendy's cheeks as she described what her son looked like, what he had been wearing. She wished she was just having a bad dream. But this terrible afternoon was real.

When the police left, Wendy turned to Glenn. "No one can help him now but God," she said. "I'm going to call the church and ask the people there to pray for his safe return."

"That's a good idea," Glenn said. He was trying to be brave, but Wendy knew he was as frightened as she was.

She phoned the church, and the lady who answered promised to ask everyone to pray for Aaron's safety right away. Then Wendy went outside again. Pacing back and forth, she looked at her watch. Six-twenty. Aaron had been gone for over three hours! "God, please send help," she murmured.

Almost immediately Wendy saw two blond girls, about eleven or twelve years of age, riding bicycles slowly down the sidewalk. As she walked toward them they stopped, as if they had been coming to see her all along. "Girls," Wendy began, "I'm looking for a little boy. . . ."

One of the girls nodded, as if she knew all about it. "He has red hair," she said, smiling.

"And a red-and-black bike," said the other.

Hope leaped within Wendy. "You've seen him?" she cried.

"He's playing with some children in a backyard," the first girl said. "I have the phone number of the house there."

"The phone number?" Wendy could hardly believe it.

"Yes." The girl recited the telephone number. She was smiling so sweetly at Wendy that she made Wendy relax a little.

"Glenn!" Wendy turned and ran into the house. "These girls know where Aaron is!" Quickly, before she could forget, she dialed the telephone number.

"Why, yes," said the woman who answered. "There's a little boy in our backyard who matches that description." She gave Wendy her address, and Glenn immediately ran out to the car to go get Aaron.

When his father picked him up, Aaron was surprised to learn that so many people had been looking for him. His friends had been playing elsewhere, so he had simply ridden his bike across several streets until, on the other side of the subdivision, he'd found some new kids to play with. Had two of them been blond girls, about twelve? No. Aaron was sure there had been no such girls. Nor had he told anyone there his name or where he lived.

How had the girls known where Aaron was, or the phone number of the house? And how did they find Wendy? Even stranger: although many people in Aaron's neighborhood had been out looking for him, flagging down passersby and stopping children to ask for information, no one remembered seeing the pair of girls at all.

Wendy never saw the girls again. But she knows who they were. At exactly six-twenty, her church community had prayed for Aaron's safety. And just a moment later the little messengers had appeared, bringing—as they always do—good news and tidings of great joy.

"It is very important to pray for others, because when you pray for someone, an angel goes and sits on the shoulder of that person."
—THE VIRGIN MARY, SPEAKING TO THE CHILDREN AT
MEDJUGORJE IN THE FORMER YUGOSLAVIA

A Helping Hand

Two-and-a-half-year-old Joey was an active child. From morning to night, he ran, climbed, and jumped. Life was a glorious adventure—so much to see and do and explore!

Of course, it's difficult to keep such energetic children safe. Joey would act first and think later. But his mother, Susie, had rules, and most of the time her little son did his best to obey them.

One Saturday morning Susie was running errands in the car; Joey was strapped in his car seat behind her. As she drove down a particularly busy street Susie noticed a garage-sale sign.

"Oh, good!" She loved garage sales, so she pulled over and parked the car directly across the street from the sign. Carefully, she opened the driver's side door into the traffic, got out, closed the door, and came around to the sidewalk.

Leaning inside, Susie lifted Joey out of his car seat and stood him on the sidewalk next to her. "Stay right here, honey," she reminded him.

Joey knew the rule about standing next to Mommy so he wouldn't get hurt or lost while she locked the car door. But there were so many exciting things to look at, and before Susie realized it, Joey darted around her, between the parked cars, and out into the street.

He was almost to the center line when Susie looked up. "Joey!" she screamed. A truck was bearing down on him, coming far too fast to stop in time. A woman across the street at the garage sale saw what was happening and screamed, too. Susie started to run.

But as she dashed into the street she suddenly realized that Joey wasn't there any longer! Instead, he was standing against her car, facing the traffic, his arms outstretched along the car's side. As if he had been *placed* there. As if someone was shielding him. . .

How had this happened? She was too grateful to wonder. "Oh, Joey!" She gathered her little boy into her arms as she wept with relief. "Don't you *ever* do that again!"

It took a moment before Susie felt composed enough to walk across the street, and when she did, she clutched Joey's hand very tightly. As she approached the garage sale the woman came toward her. "When I saw that truck coming, I screamed. . . ." she began.

"I did, too." Susie nodded.

"He's such a lucky little guy," the woman went on. "Imagine what would have happened if that man hadn't pushed him out of the way."

Susie stopped, perplexed. "Man? What man?"

"He was older, and very tall," the woman explained. "I assumed he was with you, because he grabbed your child from the middle of the street, swung him over to the side of your car, and stood in front of him."

"But what happened to the man?" Susie asked. "Where did he go?"

The woman looked around, her face puzzled. "Why, I don't know. He was *there*, and then he wasn't."

Susie was getting a funny feeling in her stomach. She knew very well she and Joey had been alone all day. Nor had she seen any man nearby. And yet, how had Joey ended up safely sheltered against the car?

"Each night I remind Joey to thank his guardian angel for keeping him safe," Susie now says. She does the same thing when she prays, too.

Veronica, a teacher in Utah, was driving to school one fall morning down a straight road bordered by fields. There was a white van ahead of her. Farther down she could see several eleven- or twelve-year-old boys ready to cross the street to go wait at a bus stop. "They had plenty of time," Veronica explains. "The van and I were far away from them."

Suddenly a car zoomed past Veronica on the right. Horrified, she realized that the boys were now in the middle of the street up ahead. All but one had already passed the center line; the last boy was slower. He obviously knew he had enough time to cross in front of the van and Veronica. But his view of the speeding car to her right was blocked—and Veronica realized that it would hit him just as he passed the van!

"I felt so helpless—I was too far away to do anything, or for him to even hear if I honked my horn," Veronica says. So she started to pray. And what she saw next is hard to describe.

"It was as if an arm literally pushed the boy from behind. His back arched, his head was thrown back, and his feet seemed propelled forward by someone behind him," she says.

In a second or two, the boy was safely on the sidewalk! He was looking back to see who had pushed him as Veronica sped by. "I will never forget the shocked expression on his face as he realized that there was no one behind him," Veronica says. No one he could *see*, that is.

Six-year-old Eileen and her older sister Dawna were best friends, but that didn't mean that they didn't argue a lot, too. They were arguing now as they walked home from school together. "I'm going to *tell* on you!" Dawna stuck her tongue out at Eileen as the two approached a street they had both crossed hundreds of times before.

It was a busy street, and Eileen should have been more careful. But sometimes Dawna made her so mad! All she wanted to do was get away from her sister's teasing, so she darted out into the middle of the street ahead of Dawna. Cars stopped in both directions, but suddenly Eileen heard brakes screeching. Dawna screamed, and Eileen looked back at her sister.

"Eileen!" Dawna's hands were at her mouth, her eyes wide with terror as she stared at Eileen. Why? What was the matter with Dawna?

Suddenly Eileen felt a strong hand grab her by her collar, the fingers hard on her neck. And then she was flying, sailing through the air across the busy street. . . . *Thump!* Eileen landed on the sidewalk. Dazed, she sat up.

People were running toward her, and Dawna was sobbing. Why were they all so excited? A car skidded to a stop next to her, and a young couple leaped out. "Are you all right?" asked the woman.

"I—I think so. . . ." Eileen began. Things were certainly confusing. . . .

"Oh, Eileen!" Crying, Dawna sat down beside her. "You got hit by a car!"

A car? "No, I didn't," Eileen started to say.

"You did," the man told her. "We all saw it. You were hit, and you flew through the air and landed here. The driver is stopped there, and the police are coming."

Eileen looked over at a car with a teenager inside parked just behind her. The driver looked pale and shaken. "He didn't hit me," Eileen insisted.

But no one would believe her. They had all seen the same thing—a collision, Eileen thrown over car roofs and landing with a thud on the sidewalk. And yet, they all said to one another, it was odd that the little girl didn't seem to be bruised or even the least bit shaken up. . . .

The young couple drove the girls home, with the police following. Eileen's mother was terrified when everyone trooped into her living room. "Are you all right?" she asked as she hugged Eileen.

"I think you should take her to the hospital," one of the police officers suggested. "She doesn't seem to have any injuries, not even any bruises, but after all, she was just involved in an accident, and—"

"But I *wasn't*, Mama," Eileen insisted. "A hand came out of the air and picked me up, and I flew to the sidewalk. . . ."

The policeman stopped talking. Eileen's mother stopped talking. Everyone looked at Eileen. "Perhaps you are a little excited, darling," her mother said carefully.

"Maybe a blow to the head . . ." suggested the young woman.

Eileen stopped. Probably no one would believe her. But somewhere there was an angel who knew what happened. And that was all that mattered.

My Minnie

*I*t was 1980 in Atlanta, Georgia, and Tabbatha was nine years old. The historic city was under siege that summer, she remembers, but not by an army. No, the person terrorizing neighborhoods, causing parents to look nervously over their shoulders and children to have nightmares, was a murderer of children. More than twenty black children and young adults would be killed before this man was found, convicted, and sent to jail. But during that summer, no one knew exactly how the situation would end. And people—of all races—were afraid.

"I can remember the mayor on television, with a million dollars in cash sitting in front of him, offering a reward to anyone who could help capture this man," Tabbatha says. "Kids under sixteen had to be home by eight o'clock every night, and the police drove through the neighborhoods to enforce the curfew. Each week, our schools bombarded us with safety films and policemen teaching us to be wary of strangers."

Like everyone else, Tabbatha was nervous. But she was also very religious. "My mother taught me to pray when I was little," she explains. "I went to church every week. One Sunday when I was six and the preacher asked if anyone in the church wasn't saved, I got up and went to the front, to accept Jesus." Tabbatha's mother wondered if her little daughter knew what she was doing. But Tabbatha knew. "Later a youth minister told us we could pray for anything, at any time, and I did."

At times Tabbatha felt a female presence around her, as if someone special was watching her. Occasionally the presence seemed to speak to her, and Tabbatha would answer—inside her head. "I told her about my fears as well as fun things," she says, "and she would tell me, 'Don't go here,' or 'Don't do this.' I named her Minnie, and figured she must be my guardian angel."

When Tabbatha was seven, she awakened one night to see a figure in the doorway. "At first I was scared, but then I realized it was Minnie, and I was actually seeing her for the first time," she says. "We talked—the whole conversation happened inside my mind—and Minnie told me that she wouldn't be talking to me anymore, but that she would always be watching me."

And so, as that fearful summer progressed, Tabbatha worried about her safety, just as all Atlanta children did. But somewhere deep within her was a little extra confidence. After all, Minnie was nearby.

One afternoon Tabbatha was in her front yard playing football with her friends, Amanda and Michael. Michael decided to go home, so the girls climbed a tree, then rolled around lazily on the grass.

Soon a large pea-green car pulled up alongside them, and the driver looked out. "I've got some cute puppies to find homes for, girls," he said. "Want to see them?"

Puppies! Of course they wanted a peek. Both children started toward the car, but then Tabbatha paused. Something just didn't seem right. And hadn't grown-ups been telling them to be cautious about strangers?

"I don't think—" she began, then stopped in surprise. Despite all the warnings, Amanda was trotting right up to the car. "Amanda, stop!" Tabbatha shouted. Then, horrified, she watched the man suddenly reach through the open window and grab Amanda.

"Help!" Both girls began to scream. Tabbatha ran and caught Amanda around her waist, trying to drag her out of the man's grasp. She wouldn't let her friend be taken away, she wouldn't! Grimly, she hung on, still screaming. But no one came outside to help, and the man wouldn't let go! Tabbatha pulled Amanda with every ounce of strength she had, but she could feel both of them losing ground, being lifted farther up through the window. . . . They were going to end up like all those kids on the news, she realized in terror. "God, send help!" Tabbatha cried out loud. "We don't want to die!"

By now, Amanda was almost completely inside the car, and Tabbatha's waist was level with the window, her feet barely touching the ground. Suddenly she felt someone's arms going around *her* waist. Whoever it was, was pulling her hard, from behind, and she felt as though she would split in two! Then both girls went flying backward, several feet above the street, and landed on the grass. With tires squealing, the car sped away.

The girls jumped to their feet, crying loudly, and Tabbatha looked around. Had Michael come back and rescued them? No, he would have been too small to pull the two of them away from that strong, insistent man. So who had? Shocked, she realized that there was no one there. They were all alone.

Tabbatha's mother wept when she heard what had happened. "Thank God you're safe!" she kept saying as she hugged them and wiped her eyes. "Thank God!"

And thank Minnie, too, Tabbatha thought. She had always wondered if her angel was still nearby. Now she knew for sure.

A special note for children: Did you ever wonder why bad things happen to good people? Tabbatha wondered, too. Since God loves all of His children just the same, why would some be accident or crime victims and others—like Tabbatha and Amanda—be able to escape?

We don't know the answer to this question. It is one of those things that we'll understand better when we get to heaven. But many believe that at the time of death, angels shield us from any pain or fright, lifting us in their strong arms and carrying us home to God. So we don't need to be afraid.

No one should take unnecessary risks. But we can also ask our guardian angels to protect us, and keep us safe. Let's do this—every day.

Lady in the Light

It was Friday, and six-year-old Dale walked home from school alone. Although his family had just moved to their new house near Columbus, Ohio, Dale already knew the route to school. He loved being in first grade, being one of the "big kids" like his older sister. Every morning he waved good-bye to his baby brother, who had to stay home with Mom, and looked forward to showing his teacher, Mrs. Sherman, how well he was learning to read and write.

Dale was also happy because it was the end of the week, and he'd spend a lot of time tomorrow with his dad. Dale's father was an engineer for a company in Columbus, but he was also a pilot in the Air Force Reserve. Every few weeks, Daddy packed his suitcase, hugged Mom and the kids, and left to spend a weekend flying. "Pilots have to be ready for anything," he once told Dale. "So every now and then, we practice."

"Where do you fly when you're in the plane?" Dale had asked.

"Oh, lots of places." Daddy had picked up his son and continued, "But I always come home in a day or two, Dale. Remember that, in case you start to miss me."

This weekend wasn't one of Daddy's flying times, though. Dale knew it because this morning they had made plans to go fishing on Saturday. Dale smiled. Weekends with Daddy around were the most fun of all.

Now he raced into the kitchen. "I'm home, Mom!" he called, putting his papers on the counter for her to see. His teacher, Mrs. Sherman, had put silver stars on them, and Mom would hang them on the refrigerator. His dad wasn't home yet, but that was okay. He'd be here for dinner tonight, and tomorrow morning they would go fishing together.

But Daddy didn't come home for dinner. Mommy got more and more worried, but when she finally phoned the place where he worked, it was closed. No one answered. So where had Daddy gone? Dale wondered. And why hadn't he phoned? Finally, it was time for bed, and Dale began to cry. "I want to see Daddy," he told his mother.

"Don't worry, Dale—I'm sure he's fine. He'll be home soon." Mom tried to comfort him, but she looked scared, and Dale felt the same way. Daddy had never gone away like this without telling anyone. Dale felt as if his world was turning upside down.

The following morning, however, Dale awakened to see his mother at his bedroom door, a smile on her face.

"Is Daddy home?" Dale asked, jumping out of bed.

"No, honey." Mom came and put her arm around him. "Last night Daddy got called by the Air Force Reserve. He had to fly to France right away. Do you know where France is?"

Dale shook his head.

"It's very far away," his mother said. "We'll look it up on a map later."

"Will he be home today?" Dale asked.

"No. He won't be home for a while."

"How long?"

"I don't know. But when the Air Force calls their reserve pilots to active duty, they just have to go."

Dale frowned. The whole thing sounded strange. But he guessed there was nothing he could do about it. When Daddy came home, he'd explain.

But Daddy didn't come home. Days turned into weeks. A month went by and still no Daddy. Dale's mother received several letters from him, which she shared with the children. But Dale was getting a funny feeling in his stomach. Hadn't Daddy told Dale that he would *always* come home in a day or two? Then why was he gone so long this time? What if those letters were just a trick? Maybe someone else had written them to keep Dale's family from finding out that Daddy was never coming back! Maybe he had left his family. Maybe . . . Dale's stomach felt queasy now . . . maybe Daddy was dead.

Dale grew quieter. He ate very little and barely spoke at home. He wouldn't read out loud anymore in school and never raised his hand. "Dale seems to be grieving," he heard Mrs. Sherman tell his mother one day. "What has happened to him?"

"I'm not sure exactly," his mother answered. "Dale misses his father. But he won't talk to me about why he's so sad." Dale realized that Mommy didn't know Daddy had died. And he wasn't going to be the one to tell her.

Later Mommy brought Dale to the doctor, and Dale heard them talking about something called "depression." The doctor sat next to Dale and held his hand. "Your daddy is just away on a job for the Air Force," the doctor said. "You understand that, don't you?"

Dale wouldn't answer. He was angry at Daddy for dying, angry that the others pretended not to know. But if he talked about it, he would start to cry, and then Mommy would know about Daddy, and *she* would start to cry. So he wouldn't say a word.

Dale's father had been gone for more than a month when Dale went to bed one night. He lay in the darkness, with that familiar hurt, sick feeling in his stomach. Was he ever going to see Daddy again? Maybe if Dale asked God, God would let him go to Daddy. . . .

Just then, Dale saw something glowing in the corner of his room. He sat straight up in bed. What was it? As he watched, the glow became larger and more radiant. Dale saw something in its center. Why, it was a figure of a woman. But not just any woman. She looked like the pictures in a book he'd read about . . . about *angels*!

The lady moved closer to him, somehow bringing the light with her. She sat down on the side of the bed and took hold of his hand. Dale wasn't scared at all.

"Dale, listen to me," the lovely lady said. Her voice was like . . . silver, all shimmery and beautiful. "Dale, you have been very worried about your daddy, but you don't need to be afraid."

Daddy! She knew his daddy! "Where is he?" Dale asked.

"He's in France, flying with the Air Force, just as your mother told you," the lady explained. "He had to go away suddenly, and there wasn't time for him to say good-bye."

"Then . . ." Everyone had been telling the truth? His father was safe?

"I am watching over your father, Dale," the angel told him. "I'll make sure he comes home safely to you when his job is finished. You help your mother while you're waiting for him. All right?"

"Yes!" Dale let out a sigh of joy, of peace so profound that he could hardly believe it. The sick miserable feeling had gone from his stomach. He felt light and bouncy, and so incredibly happy!

The bright figure was fading now. Dale reached out for her. "Don't go." But now the room was dark. It was all over.

Dale's mother was relieved the next morning when her son jumped down the stairs and ate three bowls of cereal before running off to school. "Dale seems to be fine now," she told Mrs. Sherman when she phoned later in the day.

Mrs. Sherman agreed. "He read a whole story to the class today. I wonder what made him change?"

"I don't know," Dale's mother answered. "But I'm going to give God a very big thank-you for making my little boy well and happy again!"

She did. And just a few weeks later, Dale's father came home.

Rescue in the Snow

When nine-year-old Buddy awakened on that Saturday before dawn, there was almost two feet of snow on the ground. However, he wasn't about to let a little bad weather keep him from a most important job. Buddy had just become an altar boy and was assigned to serve the six A.M. Mass today.

When Buddy came downstairs, however, his mother was still in her bathrobe. "The roads haven't been plowed, honey," she said, peering out at the dark deserted street. "I can't drive you to church—we'd get stuck. Maybe you'd better stay home."

"No, Mom." Buddy was firm. After all, a promise was a promise. "I can walk, honest. It'll be fun."

Buddy's mother looked doubtful. It was almost two miles to church. But their little Ohio town was peaceful and safe. What harm could possibly come to her son? And she was proud that he took his responsibilities so seriously. "Well . . ." She smiled. "Be sure to bundle up."

At first, since his route was downhill, breaking a path through the new snow was fun. Buddy hiked down the middle of Main Street in the dim dawn, with no people or cars around. It seemed like a winter wonderland, all quiet and clean.

But as Buddy kept walking, the drifts seemed higher and higher. His legs began to ache. He longed to reach the church so someone there would help him in, and sit him near a heater to warm his quickly freezing fingers and toes.

Finally, Buddy came to the front of the church. Just a few more steps . . . Dismayed, he realized that the snow on the church stairs was completely undisturbed. He was the first one there.

But the journey had taken so much longer than he'd expected.

Shouldn't the priest or other people have arrived by now? Using the side of his boot, Buddy pushed the snow aside, until he could finally drag open the front door.

At last! He fell inside, then stared at the cold empty interior. By the light of the just-rising sun, he could see the clock above the door. It was already six-fifteen. He had been the only one to struggle through the snow. There would be no Mass today.

Buddy knelt in a back pew for a moment, where he began to realize just how worn-out he was. His legs throbbed from pushing through the drifts, and now he would have to do it all over again. "God," Buddy murmured, "please help me get home." Slowly he turned and went out.

The way home seemed endless, each step a struggle. For every little distance that Buddy gained, he seemed to fall back even farther, pushed by the rising wind and his own exhaustion. Although it was now light out, there was still no one about, no one to ask for shelter or help. Buddy had to go uphill, and he looked with dread at the long distance remaining.

He wasn't going to make it. He knew that now for sure. His legs had been pushing through almost waist-high snow for hours, and all he wanted to do was to lie down, to end this terrible journey and close his eyes. And that's what he would do . . .

Suddenly there was someone behind him. A large man, with tender eyes, was looking down at Buddy, smiling at him. Surely Buddy should have heard the sound of the man's boots crunching the snow as he'd walked up from behind. But there hadn't been a sound.

Buddy stared at the stranger. There was a scarf hiding most of his face, but oddly, Buddy felt no fear of him. The man said nothing. He simply picked Buddy up from behind, lifted him over his head, set Buddy on his shoulders, and began to walk.

How strong he was! And where had he come from? Buddy felt exhilarated yet peaceful, all at the same time. It seemed that he and the man were wrapped in a circle all their own, an awesome connection that Buddy didn't want to break by asking questions. Yet he would have to tell the stranger where he lived. But as they approached the house, the stranger turned and walked right down Buddy's long front sidewalk. How had he known?

They reached the porch, and the man silently lowered his head and helped Buddy slide off his shoulders. "Thank you, sir." Buddy immediately turned around for a last view.

But there was no one behind him. *No one at all.* And although Buddy could see footprints up the sidewalk to where he now stood, there were no tracks leading *away* from the porch. Buddy stood in astonishment, surveying the scene. His rescuer had gone as quietly as he'd arrived.

It took a while before Buddy realized who the stranger really was. And he hasn't seen him again. "But I don't need to," Buddy says today. "I know he's still here, ready to help me again when I need him."

Pennies from Heaven

*I*t was late October. Days were cooler and shorter, and autumn leaves rattled as they blew across the streets of Lawrence, Massachusetts. Shortly after six-thirty, as thirteen-year-old Patricia finished drying the supper dishes, the phone rang. Her older brother and sister were out, so Patricia's mother answered the phone. A few minutes later she came into the kitchen. "That was the doctor," she told Patricia. "He's calling the pharmacist and ordering a prescription for me." Patricia's mother had been bent over all week with a back problem. She had tried to ignore it, but the pain had become too great, and she needed some medicine.

Now Patricia's mother reached for her purse and brought out her last crumpled bill, a twenty. "You'll have to go to the drugstore," she told Patricia. "I know it's dark, but I need the medicine, and your dad won't be home from work until after the store closes."

Patricia drew back at the sight of the twenty-dollar bill. Money always made her nervous. Their family was not exactly poor, but they had few luxuries and the children knew that every coin was precious. Patricia hated being entrusted with such an important sum.

But Mom had dark circles under her eyes, and there was no one else to go on the errand. So Patricia reached for her coat. "The prescription is ten dollars, so please carry the change carefully," her mother added. Patricia needed no such warning. Of course she'd be careful!

Patricia ran the four blocks to the drugstore, dodging raindrops and hunching her shoulders against the increasingly strong wind. Mr. Clancy had her mother's medicine all ready. "Put that change in your pocket now, Patricia," he cautioned her.

"I will." Patricia paused at the store's exit and stuffed the ten-dollar bill way down in a pocket of her jeans that didn't have any holes in it.

It was colder on the way home, and the rain was coming down even harder. Patricia was breathless as she turned down her front walk. Her mother, who had been waiting at the window, quickly opened the door. "Here's the medicine." Patricia handed the bag to her. "And here's the change." She plunged her hand deep into her jeans pocket. And felt . . . nothing at all.

How could the pocket be empty? Surprised, Patricia checked the other pocket, then her back pockets. Nothing there. Her head started to spin. "I . . . I don't know what happened," she said, quickly searching her jacket. "The money's gone!"

Stricken, she looked up and saw doubt on her mother's face. "Don't you believe me?" Patricia cried. "I lost it, Mom . . . honest I did!"

"But how could you?" her mother cried. "If you put it in your pocket, how could it have fallen out?"

"*If?* I *did* put it in my pocket!" Patricia's eyes filled with angry tears. She knew only too well what the loss of the money would mean to her family. But what hurt even more was her mother's lack of trust. How could Mom accuse her of carelessness? Patricia turned and raced out of the house. She would go back along her route and find the money!

Tears mingled with raindrops on her face as Patricia retraced her steps.

One block . . . two . . . soon her pace slowed, and her heart sank. This was an impossible search. Darkness had fallen, with patches of fog making the path she had taken even dimmer. Gusty wind swirled damp leaves against her, and drizzle dripped on her hands and down her collar. She would never find the lost money.

Then Patricia remembered a story she had just read, about guardian angels. Were they real? Did they help people? Patricia was approaching the only dim streetlight on the block. "God," she prayed, "please send your angels to find the money for me. Please . . ."

Just then Patricia heard a voice. It was not outside her head but, somehow, inside. "Stop!" the voice said firmly.

Too surprised to object, Patricia stopped.

"Look down," the voice said.

Again Patricia obeyed. She was next to the streetlight now, and right near the curb was a small mound of wet dead leaves. Patricia took a step toward the mound, then another step. The light was faint, but . . . She could hardly believe her eyes. Sitting on top of the leaves was a ten-dollar bill.

It *had* to be her money. But in this wet and windy night, how could it have landed so precisely, in the *only* area with enough light for her to see it?

Patricia's mother was delighted to receive her change. But Patricia was happy about something else. Sometimes life was hard, and she had to do scary things. But now she knew she'd never have to do them alone.

Q: Do the angels solve *all* our problems, like magic?

A: No, sometimes God wants us to solve problems by ourselves. That's how we learn and grow throughout our lives. But the angels love us very much, and we should always ask them for help when we need it.

Angel of Mercy

Michelle, who lives in Canada, had just turned six. She, her dad, and her uncle Jimmy had attended a family party at a relative's house. Michelle's mother had stayed home because she was expecting a new baby soon and wasn't feeling well.

Now the party was over, and it was very late. "Michelle, it's past your bedtime," Daddy pointed out as they pulled away from Grandma's house. "Why don't you try to go to sleep?"

Jimmy was sitting up in front with Dad, so Michelle had the backseat to herself. She took her dad's advice, stretched out, and soon fell fast asleep.

There was very little traffic, and Michelle's dad drove carefully. But as he approached an intersection, a car drove across it, right through a red light.

The two cars crashed, and since no one was wearing a seat belt in Michelle's car, all three were thrown out. Michelle's father landed first, and Jimmy fell on top of him. Michelle flew across both of them and landed nearby. But for some reason, she slept right through it!

Hearing the screech of brakes, people came running out of their houses, and someone called the emergency rescue units. Michelle awakened briefly in an ambulance. What had happened? She could hear sirens in the distance and the attendants talking to her. "Michelle. Michelle, can you hear us?" they asked.

But Michelle was too sleepy to answer. She closed her eyes again, and everything was black.

There had been several accidents that night, and so the hallways of the hospital were packed with stretchers. Someone laid Michelle on a cot in a corridor until a doctor could examine her, and someone else phoned Michelle's mother.

Michelle was frightened when she finally awakened. Vaguely, she remembered an accident, the sound of a crash, and broken glass. Where were her dad and Jimmy now? Had they been hurt? She started to cry. No one was taking care of her, or answering her questions. Oh, how she wanted her mother!

Just then Michelle spied a little old lady in a shabby fur coat making her way down the corridor. "I'm looking for my grandson," Michelle heard her explain to one patient. The woman came closer to Michelle, and then stopped and looked down at her.

Why, the lady looked like Michelle's great-grandmother, her favorite relative! Through her tears, Michelle could see that this was not really Grandma. Yet somehow, the lady seemed . . . familiar. On her face was a look of tenderness.

The lady patted Michelle on the cheeks and smiled at her. "You're going to be fine, little one," she said. "There's no need to be frightened."

Immediately Michelle stopped crying. She closed her eyes for a minute, to feel the peace that had started to warm her inside. When she opened them, the old lady was gone.

"Michelle!" Just then her mother ran up to the stretcher. "Are you all right?"

"I think so," Michelle said. "The lady made me feel better."

"What lady?" her mother asked.

"That grandma in the old fur coat," Michelle said. "She was just here."

Michelle's mother got a strange look on her face. "You must have been bumped on the head," she told Michelle gently. "I've been standing at the other end of the hallway for a while, waiting for permission to come to you. I could see you the entire time. And no one stopped at your stretcher. No old lady ever came down the corridor."

Michelle and Jimmy only needed a few stitches. Michelle's dad had worse injuries, but he recovered, too. Today, they wear their seat belts whenever they get into a car.

No one at the hospital ever saw or identified Michelle's elderly visitor. But Michelle thinks she knows who the lady was.

When the Wind Blows

Twelve-year-old Garry was happy growing up in Texas, except for one thing: every so often, rainstorms would come barreling across the open plains, bringing thunder, lightning, and sometimes even tornadoes. Garry had always been frightened of wild weather, and whenever a storm came, he would start to cry. Although he wasn't a little kid anymore, his fear seemed to be getting worse instead of better.

One afternoon when Garry was alone at home, rain began to fall.

Soon the gentle patter on the rooftop changed to hail. Garry turned on the television. "There's bad weather all around us," the forecaster advised. "Hail and high winds, even a few tornadoes in the area."

Garry was scared. *Tornadoes!* Quickly he phoned his father. "Dad, please come get me and take me to Mom. She's working at the store!" he pleaded.

"Calm down, Garry. . . ." Dad began.

"Dad, please . . . I just want to be with Mom!" Garry blinked back tears as thunder crashed outside the window. His heart had started to pound frantically.

"I'll be right there," his father assured him.

Ten minutes later his father drove up, and Garry scrambled into the seat. Dad pulled away from the house. "This will blow over soon, son," he said, trying to calm Garry. But the sky was almost black now, and with each mile, Garry became even more terrified.

When they reached the store, Garry leaped out of the car and tore through the front door. Garry's mom was waiting on a customer, and she looked up, surprised. "Garry!" she said. "What are you doing here?"

"Dad drove me," Garry gasped. "Mom, there's a tornado coming!"

"Honey, you're white as a sheet! I'm sure it's going to be fine. Let's go and check it out just to be sure." Quickly, his mother and the other customers went outside.

Garry followed them to the door, then froze. Behind his mother, way in the distance, he could actually see a funnel cloud! Blindly he raced back through the store, pulled open the heavy door of the walk-in refrigerator, and threw himself inside on the floor. He knew his mother and the customers were right outside, but their nearness gave him no comfort. All he could do was lie there in the cold darkness, trembling.

Then Garry sensed that he was not alone. There was something in the cooler with him, something warm and quiet . . . and wonderful. Instead of terror, a feeling of peace began to flow through him. He could hear the thunder, the wind howling, but somehow it didn't matter anymore. Then a voice spoke to him. "Don't be afraid, Garry." It sounded like a man's voice, and it was the calmest, most loving sound he had ever heard. "There's no need to be afraid."

The words hung in the air. *No need to be afraid* . . . Garry was silent, longing to hear more. But the message was over.

And yet, it was just beginning. Because, from that moment, Garry

completely lost his fear of storms. In fact, today when a tornado siren blows and Garry has to take cover, he doesn't mind at all. "I think the voice was my guardian angel, helping me to get through my fear," he says. "I've never heard the voice again, but I'll never forget it."

Visitors from Above

Nine-year-old Ashley's church youth group had been busy through December, rehearsing for the annual Christmas pageant. All the kids were involved in some way, either painting scenery or learning to dance or sing. There had been many late rehearsals, and many missed meals. On the night of the performance, everyone was excited. "We all said a prayer backstage before the show began, asking God to help us perform well," Ashley recalls. The chil-

dren could hear their parents and friends filling the church. This night was going to be special!

Being one of the younger kids, Ashley didn't have too big a role. When it was her turn, she and some of her friends walked down the center aisle, recited a few lines of poetry, and then sang a song with the choir, just as they had practiced. Soon their part was over, and Ashley went off the little stage. But now she was puzzled. Where should she go to watch the rest of the pageant? She knew where her parents were sitting in the audience, but she didn't want to cause a distraction by climbing over people to reach them.

Ashley's church has a rear balcony that runs the width of the building. Right in the middle, there is a classroom, with a screen that lets people look down on the pews without being seen. "That's where I'll go!" Ashley said to herself. Quietly she went down the side aisle to the back of the church and tiptoed upstairs. The classroom with its screened opening would be the perfect place to peek down from.

Ashley entered and stood still for a moment. The room was completely dark, since any lights would disturb the children on stage. She had thought she was alone, but now, as her eyes got used to the dimness, she saw a figure kneeling on the pew under the screen. The figure was leaning forward, watching the performance with obvious interest.

"He—(I think it was a he)—was wearing a loose robe, which covered him completely while he knelt," she says. "And he had shoulder-length hair." The figure reminded Ashley of a picture of Jesus that hung in the church. But how could that be? No, it must be one of her friends, someone who'd also wanted a better view of the pageant. "Hi," Ashley said softly. "Who are you?"

Slowly, the figure turned around and looked at her. Ashley couldn't see his face at all, but she felt very calm and trusting. As she stood waiting for an answer the figure simply faded away.

Impossible! Ashley went to the pew and peered under it. Nothing. She looked all around the darkened room. No one had passed her to go out, but no one was there any longer.

Ashley didn't tell any of her friends about what she saw, just her mom and dad. "But I wasn't at all afraid," she says. "I felt like I was honored. I thought it was neat that someone from heaven would come to watch our show."

Ashley only saw her heavenly visitor once. But Steven had a different experience. Steven learned to speak in complete sentences when he was very small, "which was fortunate," his mother says, "because one morning, when he was about eighteen months old, he had something special to tell us."

"A ball of light came through my window last night," Steven reported as he ate his cereal.

"A ball of light?" Steven's mother stopped buttering her toast and looked at him.

"Uh-huh. And it turned into a lady."

"Hmm." Perhaps Steven had just been having a dream. But he seemed so serious.

"The lady stayed and talked to me," Steven went on. "She showed me things."

"What things?" Mommy asked.

Steven shrugged and asked instead, "Can I have some toast?"

That was the end of the conversation—at least *that* conversation. But as the weeks passed Steven continued to talk about his visitor. She came frequently—not every night—usually moving through his closed window in a large round circle of light, which illuminated the whole room. Steven began to draw pictures of her for his parents to see. His lady didn't have wings or a halo, but she was very beautiful. "Who is she?" Steven wondered.

"Ask her what her name is," his mother suggested.

Steven did. The lady's name, he reported, was Marigo. She said she loved him, and was an angel.

Steven was surprised that his parents could not see Marigo. One night his mother awakened. It seemed as if Steven had called her, although she hadn't actually heard his voice. "Was that Steven?" she asked her husband.

"No." Steven's father yawned sleepily. "You must have been dreaming."

Still, Steven's mother got up and tiptoed to her son's door. The room was quiet and dark, and Steven lay in bed with his eyes closed. She was about to turn away when suddenly her son spoke to her. "Did you see her just now, Mommy?" he whispered. "It was Marigo."

"No, honey, I didn't," his mommy answered.

Steven sat up, frowning and confused. "Am I asleep when I see her?" he asked.

Steven's mother didn't know what to say. She couldn't see Marigo at all. But maybe some children could see things, wonderful things, heavenly things, that grown-ups couldn't.

Until Steven was almost four, Marigo visited him frequently. Then one day Steven told his parents that he wouldn't be seeing the angel again. "She told me everything I needed to know," he said. What exactly was that? Steven was not sure. "But I think I will remember when I'm supposed to," he explained.

Today Steven still misses Marigo and wishes he could see her. But he knows she is near. One afternoon when he and a friend were playing in a tree house twelve feet above the ground, Steven slipped and fell out of it. He landed on his face, but he didn't break his nose. In fact, there wasn't a bruise on him anywhere. "Maybe Marigo caught you," his mother suggested.

Steven smiled. "I think she did."

The Bible's Book of Joel (3:1) says, "I will pour out my Spirit upon all of you. Your sons and daughters will prophesy; your old men will dream dreams; and your young men will see visions."

Steering Clear

When Beth's mother went to visit a friend, she took Beth, age five, and Beth's two little sisters along. The girls played in the big backyard all afternoon, until it was time to go home.

Their car was parked in front of the house and faced down a long steep street. Mommy strapped Beth and three-year-old Meg into the backseat and put ten-month-old Amy up front in her car seat. Then Mommy got in behind the steering wheel.

"Oh!" she exclaimed suddenly. "I forgot my coat. I'll be right back, girls." She slipped out the car door, closed it, and hurried back to the house.

A minute passed. Then another. Beth sighed. Mommy was probably saying good-bye to her friend again. Beth knew she wasn't supposed to get out from under the seat strap, but sometimes grown-ups talked for *so* long. She and Meg wiggled out and got down on the floor in the back to play with their dolls while they waited.

Another minute passed, and then Beth felt the car move forward. Had her mother gotten back inside? She looked up, but she couldn't see the back of her mom's head or even hear the sound of the engine. Beth stood up. Horrified, she realized that the car was rolling down the hill, all by itself! Amy had somehow gotten out of her car seat, crawled across to the driver's seat, and shifted the gears. Ahead of them, about fifty yards away, the street ended, and a river began! They were headed directly for it!

"My babies!" Beth heard her mother scream behind them. Amy started to cry, too, as the car picked up speed. Beth saw a neighbor, who had been cutting his lawn, run toward them, but the car was going too fast for him to reach it.

"Mommy! Mommy!" Beth cried. What if the car rolled into the lake?

None of them knew how to swim. What should she do? What *could* she do?

Then, as she stood clutching the top of the backseat, Beth saw the steering wheel begin to turn very slowly to the right. There was no reason for it to move; the street was quite straight, and by now the car was traveling very fast. Yet, through her tears, Beth watched the wheel turn farther and farther and farther . . . as if someone was steering the vehicle off the steep hill.

Soon the car left the pavement and bumped along a grassy strip, moving slower and slower. Then it plowed into a small tree, and stopped.

Beth pushed the back door open, got out, and started running up the hill. "Oh, Beth!" Breathlessly, Mommy and the neighbor reached her at the same time. Mommy gathered Beth into her arms while the man and Mommy's friend ran to the car and pulled Meg and Amy out.

Mommy was now crying as hard as Beth. "Thank you, God!" was all she could say as she hugged each daughter, amazed that they had not been hurt.

For, despite the bump against the tree, none of the girls had sustained any injuries. In fact, as Beth realized afterward, even though baby Amy was no longer in her car seat, she hadn't even bounced around at all. She had

stayed quietly on the driver's seat, as if a cushion was around her, sealing her in.

It was only later that Beth told her parents about the steering wheel and how it moved. "Do you think an angel was driving?" she asked.

Her mommy and daddy didn't know what to say. But what other answer could there be?

Angels on Guard

Zack was born five weeks too soon. He came down with pneumonia and became so ill that he had to be airlifted to another hospital. There, the doctors told his distraught parents that Zack would probably die. One physician, however, decided to try a new drug, and slowly Zack began to improve. Eventually, his parents, June and Kenneth, were able to bring him home from the hospital.

Although Zack ate and slept well, he was still frail, and his parents worried about him all the time. What if he got pneumonia again? What if he didn't eat properly and lost weight? June especially found it difficult to sleep. She was always afraid that something might happen to Zack if she wasn't watching.

One afternoon when Zack was about four months old, June put him in his crib for a nap. She was so tired that she decided to lie down on the bed right next to him. She closed her eyes. It felt so good to relax. . . .

Then, as if from a distance, she heard voices. A man and a woman were talking to each other. It sounded as if they were sitting on her front porch, just a room away. June couldn't understand every word, but they were definitely talking about Zack. They discussed how sick he had been, and they seemed very concerned about him.

The voices must belong to Zack's grandparents, June decided. They had probably stopped by for a visit. June got up, went to the front door, and opened it. But there was no one on the porch.

Puzzled, June looked in the yard and around the side of the house. "Mom!" she called. "Dad? Are you here?" But there was no answer.

Had she been dreaming? But the voices had sounded so *real*. June went back to bed.

As she lay there she heard the same two people talking, again on the porch. This time June leaped off the bed, ran to the front door, and flung it open.

Again, the porch was empty.

June didn't tell Kenneth about her experience. She thought the strain she was under must be making her imagine things. She continued to hover over Zack, worrying about his health, afraid that he wouldn't grow as other babies did.

A few months passed. One night, June and Kenneth were asleep; Zack was in his crib in the same room. Suddenly June awakened. The room was dark, but she was able to see two figures peering over Zack's crib. As she watched, their outlines grew brighter. Each seemed to be wrapped in a foggy sort of glow. June couldn't see them clearly, but it appeared that one was a man and the other a woman. Instead of being fearful, June felt fascinated and relaxed.

As she watched, the man reached in through the bars of the crib and gently patted Zack on the head. "Yes, there's Zack," he said, turning to the woman. "He seems to be doing fine now. Isn't that nice?" The man's voice sounded familiar to June. Why, it was the same voice she had heard that day on the porch!

The figure of the woman nodded. Then she raised her hand, as if in blessing over the sleeping baby. Somehow the images seemed to vaporize, and suddenly the room plunged into darkness again.

June lay awake for the rest of the night, wondering about what she had seen. When she told Kenneth about it the next morning, he smiled. "I didn't tell you before," he said, "but one evening when I was in bed, I saw lights over Zack's crib. They made me feel comforted, somehow, as if angels were watching over our son."

Of course! Now June realized who the strangers had been. And from that point on, she and Kenneth stopped worrying about their little boy. "I don't know why these beings chose to visit Zack, and to let us be aware of them," she says, "but we feel honored. Zack continues to thrive, and we thank God for His constant care."

Three-year-old Joe and his family had recently moved to a new house. Joe missed his old bedroom, with its familiar wallpaper and the interesting shadows the trees made on its ceiling. Maybe he would get used to things someday, but right now he was sad, a little confused, and very lonely. What made things even worse was that Mommy and Daddy and the older kids didn't seem to notice how he felt. Everyone was busy fixing up the new house, and getting settled.

"Stay out of my stuff!" his brother would tell him.

"Joe, I'm busy now. Go and play in the yard," his mother would say. No one paid any attention to him.

One night, after Joe had gotten into a fight with his sister, his mother gave him a quick bath and put him to bed. "No, no!" Joe protested loudly. Although it was dark outside, he knew it was too early to go to sleep.

But his mother wouldn't relent. "You've been especially naughty today, Joe," she told him. "You'll just have to stay here." She closed the door with a little slam, plunging Joe's bedroom into darkness.

Standing in his crib, Joe cried angrily. It wasn't fair! Didn't they know that he was only quarrelsome and difficult because he felt uprooted, lost in this large and unfamiliar place?

All of a sudden Joe felt something soft rubbing against his bare legs. He looked down. Why, it was a cat! A gray tabby cat was in his crib, rubbing against him, purring in the nicest way. And—Joe rubbed his eyes in astonishment—there was *another*, smaller cat on his other side. She was black, with pretty green eyes that seemed to wink at him.

Cats! Joe had *always* wished he could have a cat. Where had they

come from, and how had they gotten into his crib? Joe reached down and put his hand on the gray tabby. Her fur was like velvet, softer than the nicest plush toy he had ever owned. "Kitty, how did you get here?" he asked.

Then, although he had heard no sound, Joe looked up again. Standing in front of him was a chubby little gray-haired woman. She was wearing a flowered housedress and carrying a large purse, as if she had just stopped by his room on her way to the store. She was looking right at him, and on her face was a loving smile. Joe had never seen her before.

Astonished, he realized that although his room had been dark, and no lights were turned on, he could see the cats and the old lady clearly. It was as if daylight had come into the room along with his visitors. The cats continued to purr and rub against him. Then, the lady came a step closer, reached into his crib, and picked him up. "It's all right, sweetheart," she murmured, patting his back. "Everything is going to be just fine."

The lady felt soft, and Joe relaxed against her, his arms around her, his head on her shoulder. Who was she? She seemed to know all about him, how sad and lonely he had been, how much he longed to be understood and soothed. Joe sighed in contentment. All his fear seemed to evaporate within the shelter of her arms.

The lady rocked him for what seemed like a long time. Then she put

him on the floor and let him play with the cats. Their purring filled the room, and Joe giggled as they jumped on and off his lap, their smooth tails caressing his cheeks. He felt peaceful, even happy. Everything *would* be all right. He knew it now for sure.

But his eyes were growing so heavy. He needed to close them for just a few moments. . . .

Joe awakened in his crib early the next morning and looked around in wonder. Had his visitors been just a dream? But as the days passed he felt strangely serene, hopeful, and calm. "I'm glad you are finally adjusting to our new house, Joe," his mother told him one day. "You're behaving so much better now."

Joe knew why, but he wouldn't tell. He liked having his very own secret, the knowledge that some special angels were watching over him, even at night.

According to an old American folk saying, when babies smile in their sleep, they are listening to the voices of angels!

Heavenly Housekeepers

When eight-year-old Mehul's grandmother died, his family returned to India for her funeral. Mehul didn't know Grandmother very well, because she had never come to live with them in New York. But she often wrote him letters, and he enjoyed talking with her on his visits back to India. Now he would not see her again. The thought made him sad.

He looked around Grandmother's house. It would soon be filled with relatives who had come for her funeral. "Is Grandmother in heaven now?" Mehul asked his mother.

Mehul's mother was fixing food to serve after the church services were over. She was tired after their long trip to India, and distracted about the arrangements. "Your grandmother was a good woman," she said as she sliced some bread. "I am sure she is in heaven."

"Can she see the angels?" Mehul asked. Lately, he had been very interested in angels.

Mehul's mother put down the knife. "Mehul," she said quietly, "I think it would be a good idea for you to go next door to the church and say a prayer for Grandmother before everyone else gets there. Maybe it would help you to calm down."

Mehul thought he was calm enough already. But he knew his mother was sad, so he went outside and down the path to the quiet little brick church that he and his family attended when they visited India. He would sit in the familiar surroundings and think about Grandmother, he decided. Better still, he would ask the angels to find her in heaven, to show her around and take special care of her, since she was new there.

Mehul opened the church door and walked in. Then he stopped, horrified. The church was ruined!

"Oh, no!" Mehul could hardly believe his eyes. Broken candles lay scattered across the floor. Someone had written swear words on the walls in dark letters. Things on the altar were knocked over, and the cross was split in half.

Mehul stared in dismay. Why would anyone do such a thing, especially to a church? Especially when a funeral would start in just a few moments? It made him feel sick just to look at the mess. How could his family say good-bye to Grandmother in the middle of this?

Turning, he ran the short distance home. "Mama!" he shouted, bursting into the kitchen. "Someone has wrecked the church! There are plants overturned, candles broken. . . ."

One of Mehul's aunts had just arrived. "Vandals must have done it!" she cried. "There have been several public buildings damaged recently. Oh, what will we do?"

Mehul's mother threw her apron onto the table. "Show me, son," she said, and followed Mehul out the door.

Seconds later, Mehul pushed open the church door. "Look, Mama!" he cried. Mehul's mother stopped. "Look at what?" she asked.

Mehul stared in astonishment, blinked, and stared again. He could hardly believe his eyes. The church was now in perfect order. Wax candles stood straight and tall and unbroken in their polished brass holders. The cross was back on the wall. No bad words marred the smoothness of the walls. All the debris was gone.

"Mehul, how could this be?" his mother asked. "If there was a mess here . . ."

"There *was* a mess!" Mehul declared. "I saw it!"

"Then who could have cleaned it up, in just a few seconds?"

No one, Mehul admitted. That is, no one except a heavenly cleaning crew.

A warm feeling came over Mehul. He could almost see the glow of halos reflecting off the shiny candlesticks. For hadn't he just been talking to the angels, asking them to take care of things?

He knew now that they were watching over Grandmother, *and* his whole family.

Invisible Angels

*I*ra was attending summer camp in the Catskill Mountains. He knew he should be grateful that he could spend some time in this beautiful area. Instead, he felt uncomfortable, because he just didn't fit in with the other boys. They traveled in loud, intimidating gangs, making everything an aggressive contest. Ira was shy, and he longed for just one or two pals who would share his interests and accept him.

One evening, feeling especially lonely, Ira walked away from the dining hall and watched the sun slip toward the horizon. How he wished he wasn't so quiet and reserved . . . yet how could he be anything else but the way God had made him? Ira was confused. *God, where are you?* he thought.

He had been walking for some time down a path into the woods. Now he stopped near the edge of the lake. The sun was gently setting, leaving pink and golden trails in the blue sky. Ira could hear nothing but a few birds chirping, and the lapping of water against the shore. He sat on a large branch and took his siddur, a Jewish prayer book, out of his pocket. Slowly, he read the familiar Hebrew words. Oh, if only he knew God was listening to him. "God, are you there?" he asked aloud.

Suddenly the woods began to rumble. Ira looked up in alarm. The trees above him were wildly waving, swaying, as if—as if they were *signaling* to him. Was a storm coming? No, the sky was still hazy and cloudless.

Ira stared at the billowing branches, and all of a sudden everything stopped. A deep hush fell over the woods. Each tree seemed to hold its breath, as if waiting. But why?

"God," Ira said aloud, "was that You? Tell me if You're near me. I really need to know!"

Once more the air seemed electric, filled with activity. Although Ira felt no breeze, above him the trees again exploded in frenzied motion, as if angels were moving them in wide impossible arcs. The limbs bent to the ground in a bow. Underneath, the earth thundered and shook. And then, again, there was immediate silence.

Ira's sadness and uncertainty seemed to drop from him like a heavy cloak, and his heart grew warm with love—and relief. For he knew that God and His angels had just come by, and left him with a special message of hope.

*R*achel had loved playing the clarinet ever since the fourth grade, and now she was in the high-school marching band. It had been hard learning to play and march at the same time; in the beginning, Rachel had taken many wrong turns and walked right into other members of the band! But now it was October, and with performances at several football games behind her, she was feeling like a pro.

The band had played a good halftime program, and the game was almost over. "Going to the party tonight?" Rachel's friend Jackie asked as she came up behind her in the band room.

"Uh-huh." Hurriedly Rachel replaced her clarinet in its case and turned toward the door. "But I've got to get home quickly to shower and change first," she said.

"Want a ride?" Jackie asked. "My mom will be here in a few minutes."

Rachel hesitated. It was already dark. But sometimes Jackie's mom was late, and Rachel wanted to be at the party by nine. Besides, Rachel loved to run. People up and down her street had seen her streak by ever since she was a little kid. "There goes Rachel," they would say to one another. "Have you ever seen any child run so fast?"

It had been a while since she had had a long, satisfying sprint. "Thanks, but I think I'll run home," she told Jackie now. "See you at the party!"

Rachel dashed past the football field. The game had just ended, and fans were spilling onto the quiet streets that surrounded the high school. She passed most of them in no time, and wasn't even breathing hard yet. As the crowd thinned out, Rachel put on some speed, dashing diagonally across Ninth Street and up a hill. Oh, it was great to be running, to have her hair streaming out behind her, to be feeling free and happy and—

Bamm! Suddenly Rachel slammed into what felt like a wall. The impact was so hard that she bounced back, staggered, and landed on her knees. A woman behind her saw her fall. "Are you all right?" she called.

What had she hit? Somewhat stunned, Rachel looked for a barricade blocking her path. But there was nothing there! She had collided with a huge invisible . . . something.

Just then a car full of teenagers roared over the hill and past her, so close that she could feel the ground beneath her shake, the wind strong on her cheeks. She hadn't even heard anything coming. Had she not run into the unseen obstacle, Rachel realized, she would have been in the middle of the street, right in the automobile's path. The car never could have stopped in time.

"What a close call!" The woman behind her came running up. "How fortunate that you tripped!"

Rachel got up, examining the holes in the knees of her band uniform. She hadn't tripped, but she knew the woman would never believe her.

She put out her hand. As silently as it had come, the protective barrier had vanished. Nothing was blocking her way now. But something *had*, just in time. And Rachel knew who it was. "Thank you, guardian angel," she whispered as she jogged slowly on to her house.

From the Depths

Ten-year-old Diana was spending the day at a beach in southern California with her mom and her brothers and little sister. As the children stood knee-deep in the swirling surf, their mother warned them about the undertow. "Don't go too far out," she cautioned. "You may *think* you can swim back to shore, but sometimes people get carried away by the tide, and they drown."

Diana could feel the strong pull of the current on her legs, and for a while she played carefully near the shore. Gradually, however, she paddled farther away from where Mom lay on the blanket, reading her book. Diana was having so much fun that she didn't realize how far out she had gone. Then she turned around to go back to shore.

She couldn't! The current was pulling her out to sea!

"Oh, no!" Diana swam as fast as she could, but her efforts were useless against the water's powerful push. "Mommy, help!" she screamed, and started to cry, her tears mingling with the splash of the salt water on her cheeks. But no one was near her, and no one heard. The beach seemed so far away now that the people looked like little toys. Exhausted and terrified, Diana felt herself sinking. Slowly, the sky disappeared, and everything started to get dark.

She was under the surface! Diana prayed out loud, "God, please help me." She could hear her own words clearly, yet no water entered her mouth. Now everything around her started to get brighter, almost as if the water itself was made of light. What was happening? Was this what it felt like to drown? If so, instead of being frightened, Diana felt a soft peace stealing over her. It was strange, but somehow she knew that God was very close. . . .

Just then Diana felt a strong hand gripping her wrist. Someone was pulling her firmly up, up, up, with such incredible speed that she felt almost

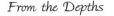
weightless. *Splash!* she broke through the waves, and somehow found herself sitting on the back of a surfboard, holding tightly to a teenage boy. "Oh, thank you for saving me!" Diana gasped.

"What are you talking about?" The boy looked back at her, completely bewildered.

"Didn't you grab me just now?" Diana asked.

"No," the surfer answered. "I was riding a wave—my last one of the day. I was approaching the shore, and then . . ." He shook his head, baffled. "Now I'm sitting on my board, back where I started, and you're here. Who are you? And where did you come from?"

As he paddled toward shore Diana explained what had happened to her. "How could this be?" the boy asked. "I didn't pull you—in fact, I didn't see you at all until you landed on my board behind me."

How had the boy suddenly gotten from the shoreline to the place out in the surf where Diana was? Who had gripped her, pulled her up, and placed her safely on the surfboard? In fact, Diana wondered, how had she been able to call out to God from *under* the surface of the water—and not get water in her lungs?

By the time Diana reached the shore, she was as dumbfounded as her rescuer. But there was one more surprise in store for her. "Mom, did you see what happened to me?" Diana made her way to the blanket.

"Yes, dear, I saw you swim in. Are you having fun?" Mom asked, smiling.

Swim in? But Diana had ridden on the back of a surfboard. She turned around, but her rescuer had disappeared.

Perhaps he was just an ordinary boy—certainly he had seemed as confused as she. But if that were so, Diana wondered, why hadn't her mother seen him, too? And surely, no ordinary boy could have found her so precisely under the waves, or pulled her to the surface with such speed and strength.

Diana had never told anyone about her adventure in the water. "God was holding on to me that day to let me know. He was real, and the only One who could save me," she says. For a long time it was a moment too special to share.

A Message for Joanie

"Joanie, wake up!"

Joanie yawned and rolled over, her eyes still shut tightly. It couldn't be morning yet. She felt as though she had just fallen asleep.

But there was that insistent hand on her shoulder again, shaking her into awareness. "Joanie, you have to get up!"

"Mom?" Slowly, Joanie opened her eyes and saw her mother's distraught face over her. It was the middle of the night! What was happening?

"Joanie, I can't take time to explain. . . ." Mom was guiding her gently out of bed, putting on her bathrobe for her as if she was a baby. "But Dad and I have to leave, and you need to stay awake and listen for the children."

Eleven-year-old Joanie was the oldest of five, and her mother sometimes called her "my extra pair of hands." Their family was very close, and Mom and Dad hardly ever did anything without explaining. This middle-of-the-night event was very odd.

"Are you awake now?" Mom was leading Joanie downstairs. In the light of the hallway she could see her father hurriedly putting on his overcoat. He gave her a worried smile.

"I'm awake, Mom, but what's going on?"

"We can't talk now, dear. We'll be back as soon as we can." Her mother grabbed her purse and followed Daddy out the door. Joanie heard their car speeding away, the sound of its engine loud in the deserted street.

What could have happened? Joanie went into the living room, slumped in a comfortable chair, and turned on the table lamp. Its rays shone on the hall clock. It was four A.M. Joanie couldn't remember ever being up at this time. How was she going to stay awake until dawn?

And then it seemed as if she was no longer alone in the room. She felt a *presence*, something warm and wonderful. Joanie was not at all afraid. *Is someone there?* she asked silently.

Do not be worried, came the answer. *God has just taken your grandmother to heaven, and now she is with Him.*

Grandma had died! Now Joanie realized why her parents had seemed so worried, and been in such a hurry. No wonder they had not told Joanie what was happening. They didn't want to leave her to grieve all by herself.

But she *wasn't* grieving. She loved Grandma very much, and knew she ought to feel sad. But there seemed to be an air of happiness, even *bliss,* in the living room.

That soothing voice had seemed male. Now Joanie heard another voice, a woman's voice. Why, it was Grandma! "I am all right, Joanie," Grandma said out loud. "Everyone will be very sad, but you must be strong and tell them that I am all right, and that I'm in heaven now."

Your grandmother was so loved, and now she is very happy, the first voice added. *She has done all she can to be ready for this day.*

Joanie was awestruck. Was she having a dream? No, she knew her grandmother's voice. And the other voice . . . it was hard to tell if it was coming from outside, or if it was speaking inside her, to her heart. But she knew—without knowing *how* she knew—that it was the voice of Grandma's guardian angel.

Then, unbelievably, Grandma was standing in front of her! She looked just like she did in a black-and-white portrait of herself and Grandpa that had always hung in their bedroom. Was this a picture, too? But no, Grandma was moving, smiling. . . . Why, she looked beautiful! She had always been a happy woman, but now she seemed radiant with joy.

"Oh, Grandma, I love you. I'm going to miss you." Joanie's eyes filled with tears. But they were not tears of sorrow. There was too much warmth, love, hope, for Joanie to be sad.

"Joanie, don't worry," Grandma reminded her again. "Tell everyone I'm happy."

Then time seemed to stand still, and the living room was bathed in a luminous glow. Joanie basked in the presence of Grandma and her unseen guardian. She didn't need to talk with them. Just being in this special place, with these special beings, was enough.

Gradually, the images faded, and Joanie could hear her baby brother stirring upstairs. It was time to see about getting breakfast.

A few hours later Joanie's father came home. "We have some bad news," he said, drawing her aside. "Your grandmother has died. We were racing to meet the ambulance at the hospital after Grandpa phoned us, but we didn't get there in time to talk to her. It happened very suddenly."

"What time did Grandma die?" Joanie asked.

"Just at four o'clock," Daddy answered.

Joanie thought of her marvelous encounter in the living room, at four o'clock. "Daddy, we don't need to be sad," she said. "Grandma's already in heaven. She's happier than she's ever been. She told me to tell you this."

No one paid much attention to Joanie in the days that followed. Everyone seemed steeped in grief. But although Joanie had loved her grandmother very much, she felt no sorrow at all. Grandma was safe with God and His angels, and had come to tell her so.

Q: Are angels the same as ghosts?

A: No, ghosts are the spirits of people who have died and, for some unexplained reason, have not yet gone to meet God. We don't know why they seem to linger here—perhaps they need people on earth to pray for them.

But like Joanie's grandmother, most people *do* meet God right after they die. When they enter heaven, they are called "saints" or "the elect." They watch over us, and sometimes, just like angels, they bring special help from heaven.

The Touch of Love

Lora was the kind of girl who just couldn't sit still.

"Calm down, Lora!" her mother always told her.

"Why can't you settle down and concentrate!" her teachers complained.

Lora didn't know *why* it was so hard for her to be quiet and learn, like the other kids in her second-grade class. And she wondered why everyone else could figure out the words and numbers on the pages so easily. To her, the words often looked like mysterious squiggly lines.

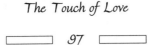
Sometimes Lora tried very hard to behave. When she caught her knee bouncing or her pencil tapping, she'd tell every part of her to CUT IT OUT! But a few minutes later her knee would be bouncing or her pencil tapping again.

At other times, though, Lora just didn't care. If people didn't like her the way she was, she couldn't help it—and she wouldn't try to change their minds. But inside, it still hurt. At night she would lie awake, praying, "God, please make tomorrow better. Please let me pay attention, and be a good girl." But nothing ever seemed to change. The next day would be the same as the one before, with Lora getting in trouble again.

One morning Lora was having an especially hard time sitting still. "Lora!" her teacher asked. "Have you finished your workbook papers?"

Lora looked at the papers. Squiggly lines. Strange marks. She couldn't figure them out. "No," she said quietly. The boy sitting across from her stared at her. The girl behind her started to giggle.

"Lora, come up to my desk, please," the teacher said.

Lora got up. Everyone in the class was watching her now, and she felt as though she would be sick. Holding her chin up, she walked to the front of the room.

"I want you to go and sit in the library by yourself for a while," the teacher told her. "Perhaps when you come back, you'll decide to complete your assignments like the other children are doing."

Slowly Lora left the classroom and walked down the hall. Her cheeks were hot with shame, and her stomach felt even sicker now. Somewhere deep in her throat she felt a burning sensation, and she wanted to cry.

She slumped down in a chair in the empty library. What was *wrong* with her? Why couldn't she learn like the other kids? Being sent to the library was a punishment, and it had already happened to her several times this year. And it never helped anyway; when she went back to class, her knee still bounced and the lines in the books still seemed to move. When her parents found out about the punishment, her mother would be mad, and her father, too—although Lora knew they were more worried than angry over her behavior.

Oh, what was she going to do? She was stupid and ugly—no wonder everyone laughed at her. Lora put her head down on her arms, and let the tears come.

Then . . . what was that? She had thought she was alone in the library. But now she felt a hand on her shoulder, a peaceful hand. It was rubbing her back, caressing her in the nicest way, somehow putting *love* into every part of her. Then a voice spoke right behind her. It wasn't either male or female, but it was the kindest voice she had ever heard. "Don't worry, little Lora," it said gently. "Everything is going to be all right."

Slowly, a feeling of comfort began to seep into Lora's heart. She felt as if the person behind her knew all about her, and loved her anyway. Who was it? She lifted her tearful face and turned around.

But there was no one there. No one in the library at all, except two older girls studying on the other side of the room.

Yet Lora could still feel the imprint of the warm supportive hand on her shoulder, still hear the sound of the voice soothing her raw spirit. "Don't worry, little Lora, don't worry. . . ."

Life was never again the same for Lora. The following year, her third grade teacher discovered that Lora had learning disabilities, and taught her how to do her schoolwork in new ways. Relieved that Lora's problems had answers, that she hadn't been misbehaving on purpose, Lora's parents made an extra effort to encourage her.

And when she still occasionally had trouble quieting down, Lora would remember the calming voice, the reassurance of that special day. She knew that an angel had come to tell her that—squiggly lines or straight, wiggly or still—she was loved.

Winged Warriors

Juan and Danny's parents were divorced, and the boys were getting ready to spend Saturday with Daddy, as they did every week. Daddy's apartment was being painted, so tonight they would be staying overnight in his new girlfriend Marguerite's apartment.

" 'Bye, Mom." Ten-year-old Juan gave his mother a big hug. Danny, age eight, did the same. The boys wished their parents were still together, but spending special time with their dad was the next best thing.

"Behave yourself." Mom smiled at them.

"We will."

It was a good day. They went with Dad and his girlfriend to the park, where they played some baseball and grilled hamburgers. Finally, after baths and some TV watching, Dad tucked them into Marguerite's king-size bed. "Marguerite and I are going outside for a walk," Daddy assured them. "You go to sleep now."

The bed was roomy and comfortable, and Juan felt himself drifting off to sleep right away. Suddenly, however, Danny poked him. "Juan! Juan!" Danny whispered. He sounded frightened.

"What?" Juan asked.

"The ceiling! Look at the ceiling!"

Juan looked up. He couldn't see anything in the dark room. "What are you talking about, Danny?"

"Can't you see the scary faces up there? They look like monsters—they're staring at me!"

Juan rolled over and closed his eyes. "Danny, you're just dreaming, that's all," he scoffed. "Go to sleep. There's no such thing as monsters."

A few moments passed. Then Danny poked Juan again. "They're still there! See them? Juan, they're so ugly! I'm scared."

Juan sighed. At this rate, he'd be up all night. "Danny, go back to sleep," he murmured. "It's all in your mind."

Another moment passed. Now Juan could hear Danny crying quietly. He rolled over again. "Danny, I'm getting mad!"

"Juan, you have to do something!" By now, Juan's eyes had gotten used to the darkness, and he could see Danny staring at the ceiling, wide-eyed with terror. Juan looked up again. There was nothing there at all . . .

. . . Or was there? Astonished, Juan saw a dim face, then another face, until the whole ceiling seemed to be filled with them. Danny was right— they were hideous, evil . . . and they looked like the pictures of devils that he had seen in books!

The faces were not moving. They seemed to be painted on the ceiling, like a mural. And yet, oddly, the scenes kept shifting again and again, showing more creatures with different expressions and poses. It was almost as if he was looking at a terrifying slide show.

Oh, they were dreadful! Juan turned away from the faces, repelled. He must be dreaming. He *had* to be dreaming! But he knew this was real.

He should grab Danny right now, jump out of bed, and escape from the room. But what if there were *more* evil beings in the living room? The boys had never been in this apartment before. What if something was terribly wrong with it?

Danny was still crying beside him. "I want my mommy," he sobbed.

Mom . . . Juan wanted her, too. And then he remembered something. "Whenever you are frightened," his mother always told them, "just ask God to send His angels to protect you."

They could do that, Juan realized. Even with devils looking at them from the ceiling, they could pray. Juan reached for Danny's hand and held it tightly. "Let's ask the angels to come," he said.

They didn't know quite *how* to ask, but special words didn't seem to be necessary. "Angels, help us," both boys murmured again and again. And as they prayed, the ceiling began to change. The ugly faces had been on a black background, but now as Juan watched intently, the ceiling faded into white. Then an angel appeared at the right corner, a large winged warrior! "Do you see it, Danny?" Juan whispered, excited.

"Yes, an angel!" Danny answered. "And look, there's another, and another . . . !"

Enthralled, both boys watched as big strong angels began to fill the air above them, again not moving, but as scenes shifting, one after another. Each scene brought more and more angels, moving from right to left across the ceiling, pushing the ugly faces to the edges of the room. *They are fighting for us,* Juan realized in awe. He knew that he was seeing something most people never glimpse: the invisible battles of the spirit world.

Slowly, slowly, the devils gave way, until just angels remained, wonderful beings who not only filled the ceiling but came down the walls, surrounding the boys with protection. Cozy and warm, the two fell into a blissful sleep.

When Juan and Daniel came home on Sunday, they told their mother what had happened. She did not laugh at them. Instead, she did some checking. Why had they been so scared! What had been going on in Marguerite's apartment?

Eventually she learned that Marguerite and some of her friends had been using the apartment for witchcraft rituals, séances, and other occult activities. These women had invited evil spirits into their lives, and undoubtedly Juan and Danny had felt their presence when they had stayed overnight.

Luckily, the boys had known what to do. "I still feel angels around me today," Juan says. "I know that, whatever happens, we can call on them for help."

. . .

A special note for children: God doesn't want any of His children getting involved in things that are frightening. Whatever your age, it's smart to avoid not only violent video games and movies, but Ouija boards, tarot cards, fortune-telling, and books about witchcraft. People may tell you that such things are only games, but they can also be doorways to danger from the dark side of the spirit world.

Remember: no one can play on two teams at the same time. And *you* want to be on the side of God and His angels. Say no to anything else.

A Cradle of Love

Eight-year-old Daniel lived in Buenos Aires, a huge city in Argentina, South America. Here, the architecture is very mixed, with high apartment buildings, like towers, next to two-story buildings, and low houses all around. Today was the day Daniel was going to attend his friend José's birthday party. He was very excited, for children here, as everywhere, love parties!

José lived just two blocks away from Daniel. The two always walked to school together, and Daniel had often played on the big terrace in the

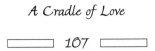
back of José's house. From the terrace, the boys could see the roofs of sur-rounding houses. A wall separated them from the building next door.

That afternoon, Daniel walked to José's house, carrying a birthday present for him. Several boys were already on the terrace. "Hey, Daniel!" one shouted. "You're just in time to play ball."

Daniel joined his pals, and the boys threw the ball around. All of a sudden someone missed a catch, and the ball sailed over the wall onto the roof of the building next door. Instantly the boys climbed up the wall and scrambled onto the roof.

"There's the ball!" Daniel saw it first, lying on top of a glass skylight. Daniel had seen such skylights before, on top of his school's roof. Skylights save energy by letting sun inside, and Daniel knew the glass they used was very hard. This large pane would hold an eight-year-old boy easily. Daniel stepped up onto the skylight, reached for the ball, and . . .

Crash! The window shattered into a million pieces. Daniel fell through it, and hurtled toward the basement floor below.

His fall seemed to take hours. Feeling as if he were in slow motion, Daniel spun upside down and around, completely out of control. Finally, he landed.

But . . . although he had fallen more than two stories, he seemed to be fine. Gingerly Daniel felt his head, arms, and legs. Nothing was broken. He sat up. In spite of all the jagged glass surrounding him, he could see only one small cut on his right arm. It didn't even hurt. *Nothing* hurt.

"Daniel? Are you all right?" His friends were shouting down from the top of the roof near the skylight.

"I think so," he called back. He slowly got to his feet, grateful but confused. Soon he heard a key turn in a door and José's parents came running in to find him.

José's mother gave him a big hug. "The people who live in this house are on vacation," she explained. "They left their key with us."

José's father was looking around. "Daniel must have landed on this chair," he said. "That's what broke his fall."

Daniel turned around. There was an old ugly armchair behind him, tilting because of a broken leg. He *had* landed on it before hitting the floor; now he remembered.

But something was very odd. Daniel realized he was in a luxurious living room, beautifully furnished. Why would such an old chair be in a room like this? Especially right underneath a skylight—as if it had been placed there just for him?

No one, not even the owners of the house, ever discovered who owned the chair, or where it had come from. "I thought it was a great co-incidence at first," Daniel says. "But now I believe my guardian angel moved that chair from somewhere else, to save my life. He was watching out for me that day. And he still does."

☐

"Lisa! Come out and skate with us!" Fifth-grader Lisa looked out her window. Her two best friends, Janice and Karen, were skating up and down Lisa's front sidewalk and calling to her. It didn't take Lisa long to grab her roller skates and cruise out to join them.

In summer, the girls skated every day. It was, by far, the most fun thing to do. They had to be careful, of course, especially when they skated fast, because the sidewalks in their neighborhood were old, with bumpy and uneven places. Tripping over a broken piece of concrete could cause a bad fall.

But that never slowed them down. "Let's race!" Janice shouted, and all three started off down the sidewalk. Lisa's long hair streamed out behind her as she built up speed. Soon she was laughing out loud. Skating was *so* much fun!

And she was winning, by at least three house widths! Lisa looked behind her and grinned at her friends. Just then she felt her back foot hit a large crack in the sidewalk.

Lisa was skating so fast that she flew into the air, her feet in front of her. Then she began to fall backward. *Oh, no!* She would land right on the top of her head, and there was nothing she could do! "Lisa!" her friends screamed behind her.

Lisa's long hair was already touching the sidewalk, and she braced herself for the impact, and the pain.

And then she felt something she hadn't expected: the pressure of two hands at the top of her back. Big hands, steady hands . . . they were pushing her back up onto her feet. Suddenly she was upright, although very unsteady and off balance. Then those hands gave her another push, this time a gentle one, and she fell forward into the soft grass.

Janice and Karen glided up, breathless and astounded. "How did you do that?" Janice asked. "You were falling upside down, and then you stood right side up again!"

Lisa wondered if she should tell her friends about those wonderful, invisible hands. She decided to do it.

The girls' eyes grew very big. "Maybe it was an angel," Karen suggested.

That's what Lisa thought, too. What other answer could there be?

Ten-year-old Lee and his two brothers loved to play on the wooden stairs that connected the first floor of their house with the second. Sometimes they slid down the steep banister. Other times they jumped from the third—even the fourth or fifth—step to the floor below. And when their mother told them to bring down the laundry from the bedrooms so she could wash everyone's clothes, the boys would do it—by dropping the clothes at the top of the stairs, and sliding on them all the way down!

When playing, Lee had to be a little more careful than his brothers. His left foot turned inward, and from time to time he would lose his balance and stumble. "Tanglefoot!" his brothers occasionally teased when they saw his bumps and bruises. Lee didn't mind being teased, but falling on those bare wooden stairs really hurt—and he was always just a little afraid of that.

One morning his mother called to him from downstairs. "Lee, hurry up! You'll be late for school!"

"Coming!" Quickly, Lee rounded the corner and started down the stairs. Horrified, he felt himself slip. His feet went out from under him, and he rolled head over heels in a somersault, crashing against the wall, then the banister, clattering helplessly down that long steep flight.

Help! He would break a bone or crack his head. Lee tried to grab the spokes in the banister to stop his wild tumbling, but he couldn't.

Then his skid seemed to stop, in midair. Why, Lee felt as though he was cushioned in a cloud. He was tumbling down the last three steps now, but they weren't hard at all. In fact, he could hardly feel them.

Bounce, bounce, bounce. Gently Lee floated to the floor, landing on what felt like a feather pillow, soft and fluffy.

Slowly, Lee stood up. He felt just fine. And there wasn't a mark on him. But there wasn't a pillow on the floor either. Everything looked just as it always did. How had Lee been so softly shielded? "I fell down the stairs," he told his mother, who had just run to him, "but it felt like someone caught me."

His mother just smiled.

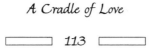
• • •

Psalm 91 (11–12) tells us about God's promise concerning angels:

For He will command His angels to guard you in all your ways;
They will lift you up in their hands, so that you will not strike your foot
  against a stone.

(Or even a stair!)

The Christmas Angel

It was a few days before Christmas in Hamilton, Indiana. Ten-year-old Kari had gone with her baby sister, Amy, and her mom on some errands, and now they were buying a few things at the grocery store. Kari was a bit tired. She would rather have stayed at home, but her mom needed her to help watch Amy.

Finally, they unloaded their items at the checkout counter. Kari looked idly around, then noticed a plastic mayonnaise jar on a shelf near the cash register. A picture of a girl was taped on it, and below that was a handwritten sign that read BETH L . . . HAS CANCER, DESPERATELY NEEDS DONATIONS FOR BONE MARROW TRANSPLANT.

Why, Kari realized, she *knew* Beth. Beth was in a higher grade at her school. But Kari hadn't known Beth was sick.

"Look, Mom." Kari pointed at the empty jar. "I know this girl."

Her mother read the sign, and her eyes filled with tears. "That poor family—they must be so worried," she murmured.

"Could we give them some money?" Kari asked. Then she remembered with dismay how tight their own budget was. There was no way Mom could spare anything, especially right now, the week before Christmas.

But Mom had just been handed several bills in change. She looked at the money for a moment, then put it all in the jar. "This is all I have," she said sadly. "I wish it were more."

Kari knew the donation was a real sacrifice. As they walked to the car she felt tears spring to her eyes. She was proud of what her mom had done.

Mom started the engine and pulled out of the parking lot. As the car headed down a dark highway, Kari closed her eyes tightly and prayed for Beth. What must it be like, having cancer and being scared?

Then Kari heard something hit the windshield. It sounded like a pebble. "Look at that!" her mother cried.

Kari's eyes popped open. A small ball of light, shining a bright silver blue, was bouncing on the outside of the front window. And then, unbelievably, it was *inside* the car, flashing and shining, getting bigger and bigger, wrapping them all in a brilliant cocoon.

Kari was astonished. The light couldn't be coming from outside, she realized; theirs was the only car on the dark road, and there were no streetlights along their route, and not even any Christmas lights. Besides, the ball was far too bright to be just a reflection. Awed, Kari watched it. It was dazzling, radiant, yet somehow joyful, too, as if . . . as if it were *dancing*. And was that the outline of a figure in its center? Kari couldn't tell for sure.

She looked outside and noticed that the whole area where they were riding seemed to be illuminated. She looked at Amy. The toddler's eyes were wide in wonder.

As quickly as the light had appeared, it vanished, and the interior of the car was completely dark again. By now Kari's mother had pulled off the road, and she turned to Kari. "You look as shocked as I am," she said. "What did you see?"

"A ball of light! It came inside the car!" Kari cried. "Mom, what was it?"

"I don't know," her mother said slowly, thoughtfully. "Maybe it was a Christmas angel, bringing us a message of hope for Beth, or thanking us for giving our money to her. . . ."

Kari thought about it. "Do angels do that? Do they bring good news to ordinary people like us?"

"They did on the first Christmas," her mother reminded her, smiling. "Why not now?"

The strange light didn't return. But this Christmas turned out to be the best one Kari's family had ever had. Even though they didn't have much money, they felt very blessed, as if the joy of the bouncing spark was still in their midst.

And when vacation ended, Kari received another gift. "How is Beth?" she asked a friend on their first day back in school.

"Oh, Beth had her transplant and she's able to come back to school today," her friend replied.

Kari was surprised and happy. She knew that not every sick person got well, especially not right away. Sometimes things like this took time, because God's plan wasn't the same for everyone.

But no matter what the results seemed to be, God *always* wanted His people to care for each other and to offer their help, even when it wasn't easy, even when it cost time or money. That was the best way to make earth more like heaven, to make every day like Christmas.

An angel of light had told Kari so.

Angelic Notes for Kids

Prayers, Songs, Poems, and More

Angel Prayers

How do you get to know a good friend? By talking with him or her. And when we talk with God or His angels, we call it "prayer."

Prayer doesn't have to be complicated. You can pray in whatever way you choose. You can talk about things that worry you, things that make you happy, or anything that's in between—and that's prayer. Or you can recite words that someone else wrote.

A great way to start your day is to ask your angel to be with you. As soon as you wake up—before you even open your eyes—you might like to say:

> Angel of God, my guardian dear,
>
> To whom God's love commits me here,
>
> Ever this day be at my side,
>
> To light and guard, to rule and guide. Amen.

(You can sing this, too. Use the tune of "Rock-a-bye, Baby.")

End your day by asking your angel to guard you while you sleep. After you turn the light out and snuggle under the covers, try one of these "good night prayers":

> Now I lay me down to sleep,
>
> I pray, dear Lord, my soul you'll keep.
>
> May angels watch me through the night
>
> And wake me with the morning light. Amen.

or

Lord, keep us safe this night
Secure from all our fears.
May angels guard us while we sleep,
Till morning light appears. Amen.

or

Matthew, Mark, Luke, and John,
Bless the bed that I lie on.
Before I lay me down to sleep
I give my soul to Christ to keep.
Four corners to my bed,
Four angels overspread:
One at the head, one at the feet,
And two to guard me while I sleep. Amen.

Here is another prayer to say anytime:

MY GUARDIAN ANGEL

Dear angel ever at my side, how lovely you must be
To leave your home in heaven to guard a child like me.

When I am far away from home, or maybe hard at play—
I know you will protect me from harm along the way.

Your beautiful and shining face I see not, though you're near,
The sweetness of your lovely voice, I cannot really hear.

When I pray you're praying too, your prayer is just for me.
But when I sleep, you never do. You're watching over me.

—AUTHOR UNKNOWN

Angel Songs

And if you'd like to sing about angels, here are two songs for you to learn:

All Night, All Day

Beautiful Angel

Moderato espressivo.

1. Guar - dian an - gel, From heav'n__ so bright, Watching be - side me, To
2. An - gel so ho - ly! Whom God sends to me, Sin - ful and low - ly, My

lead me a - right, Fold thy wings round me, O guard me with love,
guardian to be Wilt thou not cher - ish The child of thy care?

CHORUS. *(Repeat **ppp**)*
2d. time Alto bouche fermée.

Soft - ly sing songs to me, Of heav'n a - bove. Beau - ti - ful an - gel, My
Let me not per - ish My trust is thy pray'r.

guardian so mild, Ten - der - ly guide me, For I am thy child.

Angel Poems

People like to write poems about angels. Here are some you might like:

WHISPER OF ANGEL WINGS

Today I stumbled and once again
Was lifted up by an unseen hand.
What comfort and joy that knowledge brings.
For I hear the whisper of angel wings.

The guardian angels God sends to all
To bear us up when we stumble and fall.
Trust Him, my friend, and often you'll hear
The whisper of angel wings hovering near.

—AUTHOR UNKNOWN

GUARDIAN ANGEL

'Tis said we are blessed
With a guardian angel in disguise.
We do not always know them,
For they appear in any form or size.

They do arrive when needed,
In a strange, mysterious way,
Not by chance as some may think,
But on a special day.

So if you are sad with no direction
As to what course to pursue,
Just wait for your protection
From an angel meant just for you.

—MARY M. WADHAM

MY ANGELS, MY FRIENDS

I forgot about your angels, Lord,
That they stay always near
To help me through my days
When I'm feeling fear.

I forgot when I'm distressed
And anticipating harm,
That they are ever ready
To hold me in their arms.

I admit sometimes it's hard
And my human eyes don't see.
And I still *feel* alone
Even though an angel is with me.

I just need to remember
That You promised us their care.
And it just takes faith
To realize they are there.

—DONNA BOYD

Angel Stories and Legends from Around the World

In France a long time ago, the peasants had an interesting tradition. Instead of simply saying "Hello!" when they met each other, they would say, "Good day to you and your companion!" Although people couldn't see them, they thought guardian angels deserved to be greeted, too.

A holy man named John Bosco lived in Turin, Italy a number of years ago. He worried about all the homeless young men on the streets. They were tough and rude, and although John tried to bring them food and comfort, gangs of them often mugged him and stole everything he had. John was getting tired of this.

"God," he prayed one evening, "if you want me to care for the homeless, you'll have to take care of me!"

The next day, John walked toward the bad section of town, looking nervously around him. Was he going to get attacked again? Just then he noticed a large gray dog walking next to him. Where had the dog come from? John stopped, and the dog stopped, too. John began to walk, and the dog trotted alongside. The gangs watched as John Bosco and the dog made their way through the streets. No one would bother him today—not with that huge gray animal beside him! From that day on, the dog appeared whenever John traveled through a dangerous part of town, and disappeared when John Bosco was in a safe area again. John named the dog Grigio, which means "gray."

John Bosco was never mugged again, and eventually he founded a community of priests to care for the homeless. For years after his death, many of these men reported being mysteriously protected too—by a big gray dog!

Have you heard this Christmas legend? In a wintry land of the East, a little princess knelt in the snow and prayed for her father to return from a journey. Suddenly a beautiful angel appeared. "Your father is one of three wise men who have followed a star and found a savior," he said.

No one believed the little girl's account of the angel. But months later when her father returned to tell her of Bethlehem, the princess led him to the place where the angel had appeared to her. There on the ground, with snow heavy all around, one bare patch of earth remained untouched by snow—in the perfect shape of an angel.

This is why children today still make snow angels, to commemorate the birth of Baby Jesus.

The angels were present at the creation of the world. They sang and danced when they saw what God had made! (Job 38:7). That's why legends have sprung up around the theme of angels and nature. Here are just a few:

   . . . Stars are the windows of heaven, through which the angels peek.

   . . . Angels get to earth by sliding down sunbeams.

   . . . Angels play hide-and-seek among the flowers.

   . . . When a raindrop falls on your nose, you've just been kissed by an angel.

   . . . It thunders because angels are bowling!

   . . . It snows because angels are having pillow fights!

Test Your Knowledge

Q: Did you know that the word *angel* means "messenger?" What other titles do angels have?

> *A:* —Heavenly host
>
> —Guardians from above
>
> —Good spirits
>
> —Cherubim and Seraphim
>
> —Sons of God
>
> —Celestial choir

Can you think of more?

Q: Did you know there is a fish named an "angelfish"? What other things are named after angels?

> *A:* —Angel food cake
>
> —The California Angels baseball team
>
> —Los Angeles, in California (it's called "the city of angels").
>
> —The Guardian Angels street patrol

Can you think of others?

. . .

Q: What creature is called "angel of the sea?"

   A: The dolphin.

Q: How many angels can dance on the point of a pin?

   A: Millions, even billions! Angels have no bodies, so they don't take up any room.

Q: What days of the year do we pay most attention to angels?

   A: October 2 is the feast day of guardian angels. It's a time to thank your angel for all the help he or she has given you all year.

August 22 is called "Be an Angel Day." On that day, people do special— and anonymous—favors for one another.

And during December, be sure to read about Jesus' birth (the first few chapters of Matthew and Luke). Count how many times angels were involved in this wonderful event!

Resources

For Children

VIDEOS AND MORE

Timmy's Secret and *Timmy's Special Delivery*. Precious Moments animated videos ($12 each) presenting adventures of Timmy the angel and his friends. Suitable for Christmas or anytime. Also available: Precious Moments angel dolls and other angel products. Contact:

> Angels for Everyone
>
> 27766 Berwick
>
> Mission Viejo, CA 92961
>
> (714-364-5935 for order information and catalog)

Angels All Around Us. A thirty-minute video featuring dramatizations of true-life angel encounters. Contact:

> Liguori Publications
>
> 1 Liguori Drive
>
> Liguori, MO 63057
>
> 800-464-2500, Order Department.

ANGEL ITEMS, INCLUDING:

Beneath an Angel's Wing activity/coloring book (ages 4–8) $1.50

Guardian angel puzzle (ages 2–7) $1.50

Angel on my Shoulder pins $1.00

Angel medals $7.50 Contact:

> The Medjugorje Star
>
> 2627 David Drive
>
> Metairie, LA 70003
>
> (800-625-1981 for order information)

The Book of Angels. Terrie Tomko. Bible-based stories told in rhyme. $4.95 (ages 4+). *Angel of God.* Piera Paltro. Based on "Guardian Angel" prayer. $2.50 (ages 4+). *Angel of God Coloring Book* 75 cents. Contact:

> St. Paul Books
>
> 50 St. Paul's Ave.
>
> Boston, MA 02130
>
> (800-876-4463 for order information)

Pink Stars and Angel Wings. Susan Ekberg. Darling story of a little girl who meets her angel (age 4+). Fiction. $16.95. Taped version w/music $9.95. For both, add $4.50 for shipping. Contact:

> Spiritseeker Publishing
>
> P.O. Box 2441
>
> Fargo, ND 58108
>
> (800-538-6415 for order information and catalog)

My Little Angel Tells Me I'm Special. Plush doll (in assorted colors) and motivational tape set (60 minutes). Reassuring messages set to music to help children fall asleep and banish fears. $24.95 postpaid, or send self-addressed stamped envelope for more information to:

> Sutherland Communications
> P.O. Box 70
> Hansville, WA 98340

Household angel items, including art, wind socks, posters, weather vanes, and more. Send $1 for a catalog to:

> Marilynn's Angels
> 275 Celeste
> Riverside, CA 92507

BOOKS

The Alabama Angels. Mary Barwick. New York: Ballantine, 1993. $15 (age 5+). Illustrated stories of black angels at work in Alabama. Fiction.

Angels Are My Friends. Annetta E. Dellinger. St. Louis: Concordia Publishing House, 1985. $5.95 (ages 5–9). Child and grandmother discuss angels from biblical perspective.

An Angel for Solomen Singer. Cynthia Rylant. New York: Orchard Books, 1992. $14.99 (ages 8+). A lonely man meets a real-life angel. Fiction.

The Snow Angel. Debby Boone. Eugene, Oregon: Harvest House, 1991. (ages 5+) $12.95. An angel brings hope and encouragement to an entire town. Fiction.

Why Can't Grownups Believe in Angels? Marsha Sinetar. Liguori, MO: Triumph Books, 1993. $14.95. A celebration of spiritual values for all ages. Nonfiction.

For listening: A lullabye titled "Guardian Angels," words by Gerda Beilenson, music by Harpo Marx, originally recorded in 1951 by Mario Lanza, currently on a compact disc titled *Christmas with Mario Lanza.* (RCA.)

Watch for: A new operetta titled *The Singing Child* by Gian Carlo Menotti, author of *Ahmal and the Night Visitors.* A mysterious singing child visits a lonely little boy and helps his parents become more aware of his need for love and attention. Recommended for the whole family.

Also recommended: The classic opera, *Hansel and Gretel* by Englebert Humperdinck, often performed at Christmastime. Perhaps a little scary for very young children, but the music is lovely and there are many references to angels.

For Adults

Children's Letters to God. Stuart Hemple and Eric Marshall. New York: Workman Publishers, 1991.

The Spiritual Life of Children. Robert Coles, M.D. Boston: Houghton Mifflin, 1990.

Visions of Innocence: Spiritual and Inspirational Experiences of Childhood. Edward Hoffman, Ph.D. Boston: Shambhala Publications, 1992.

A Window to Heaven: When Children See Life in Death. Diane Komp, M.D. Grand Rapids, MI: Zondervan Publishing House, 1992.

When Children Ask About God. Harold S. Kushner. New York: Schocken Books, 1989.

Author's Afterword

I am always interested in hearing from children and adults who believe they have had an angel experience. You can write to me at P.O. Box 1694, Arlington Heights, IL 60006. Although I may not be able to answer each letter, I will lovingly read each one and keep it on file. If your story can be used in my future writing, I will contact you.

—JWA

JOAN WESTER ANDERSON began her writing career in 1973 and has published over a thousand articles and stories in a wide variety of magazines and newspapers. Her books include *The Best of Both Worlds; Dear World, Don't Spin So Fast*; the best-selling *Where Angels Walk*; and its recent sequel, *Where Miracles Happen*.

Joan and her husband live in suburban Chicago and have five grown children and one grandchild.